Duleepsinhji

Prince of Cricketers

by Barry Rickson

With a Foreword by John Barclay

The Parrs Wood Press
<u>Manchester</u>

First Published 2005

THE PARRS WOOD PRESS
St Wilfrid's Enterprise Centre
Royce Road, Manchester, M15 5BJ
www.parrswoodpress.com

ISBN: 1 903158 65 6

Printed by Compass Press Ltd.

I dedicate this book to my family,
my wife Jen and my three sons,
John, Robert and Edward.

CONTENTS

LIST OF ILLUSTRATIONS

(between pages 96 and 97)

ACKNOWLEDGEMENTS

I am indebted to many people for their very kind and willing help in compiling this account of Duleepsinhji's life.

In the first place I must thank David Frith for putting the idea in my mind of writing this book, even though he may not have realised how seriously I would take his words.

Tim Pearce and Christine Leighton were most hospitable in allowing me to search for material in the archives of Cheltenham College and, in fact, in drawing my attention to so much of great interest.

Elizabeth Stratton, archivist at Clare College, Cambridge University, was most helpful in providing me with information about Duleepsinhji's days as a student at the college.

Rob Boddie, librarian of Sussex County Cricket Club, and his friend Roger Packham could not have been more helpful in giving me background information. The photographs they supplied me with were fascinating, whilst their knowledge of the club's history was encyclopaedic.

Tim McCann of the West Sussex Records Office at Chichester unearthed a wonderful collection of Duleepsinhji memorabilia for me.

Keith Hayhurst has been extremely kind in allowing me access to his book collection at all times.

Cheryl McNamara at the Australian Archives in Brisbane discovered many useful documents for me.

Richard Cragg has been first-class in closely perusing the text and in giving me much sound advice.

In addition to helping substantially with the "office" work, my wife Jen has been patience personified as Duleep seemed to take over the house!

I am most appreciative of that fine Sussex Captain, John Barclay, for writing such a kind and comprehensive Foreword.

Most of all, however, I am enormously indebted to Murray Hedgcock who has been unstinting in his encouragement and assistance in so many ways. His advice has always been thoughtful and constructive, his research on my behalf exhaustive.

In conclusion, my thanks must go to the publisher, Andy Searle, who has been so patient and understanding in his dealings with me and who gave me the opportunity to trace the life story of Duleep.

PREFACE

I first had the idea of writing this book after attending a talk by David Frith, that most prolific of cricket writers. His subject had been the writing of biographies which he said only really appealed to him if there was "something a little different about the subject". He asked for suggested subjects, so I approached him at the end and proposed Duleepsinhji whom I saw as a parallel in many ways to Archie Jackson, that great Australian cricketer whose life story had already been told by David. His response took me aback a little as he said "Good idea! Why don't you do it?"

I thought about it a little but then dismissed it from my mind, until I met his colleague Murray Hedgcock and mentioned it to him. He is very persuasive and more or less bullied me into attempting the project. I was surprised that there had been no biography of him as such considering his great reputation and as the year was 2003 I felt that I had better begin so as to be ready for publication to mark the centenary of Duleepsinhji's birth in 2005.

Delving into his history through archives at his school, university college and county proved fascinating and enlightening. I found it of particular personal interest to see one of his school reports signed by his form teacher, a certain young FH Philpot who became my headmaster during all my years at Stockport

Grammar School and then signed many of my reports, although not necessarily as favourably!

His career was one of many parts, as although he will be remembered first and foremost as a great cricketer, he also achieved distinction in several other fields, most notably as his country's High Commissioner in Australia and New Zealand. There is a strong romantic side to his life as we have an oriental prince in the days when India was very much a key part of the British Empire, playing in such a beguiling manner and style which marked him as something different from the normal; in fact, to add to his charisma, there had been nobody like him since his uncle, that superb batsman at the turn of the century, the great Prince Ranjitsinhji with whom he was constantly compared. This great enchanter with the magical style was stricken at a very early age with what was in those days an almost incurable illness and died at the young age of 54. In his artistry, his delicacy of touch and in his suffering from tuberculosis he could also be called *The Keats of Cricket*, as David Frith sub-titled his work on Archie Jackson.

I hope that too many people do not object to my use of the names "Ranji" and "Duleep" instead of the fuller forms as I feel that these forms give more feeling of intimacy to the gentlemen concerned and less formality. I must say that by the time I finished I felt that I almost knew Duleep - I wish I had!

FOREWORD

by John Barclay

HOW VERY uplifting it has been, and a great honour too, for me to write a few words by way of introduction to this charmingly written and valuable book which engages the reader so movingly with the spirit of the age.

Kumar Shri Duleepsinhji. His very name suggests class, style and finesse - not for him the heavy bat and rounded forearms of the modern cricketer. Rather there would have been a delicacy of touch - the late cut feathered away past slip patiently using the pace of the ball; all wrist and elegance, shirt sleeves tidily buttoned down.

How easy it is to get carried away. Of course, I never saw Duleep play; there can only be a few left who did. He died young at the age of 54 in 1959 when I was just five years old and learning to swim. At that stage cricket had scarcely had the chance to take over my life. It did though, and it was not long before I became entranced by heroes present and past. Hutton, Hammond, Hobbs, Compton and later May, Cowdrey and Trueman were just a few of them - batsmen for the most part, but none from Sussex so I wasn't sure they really counted.

By contrast though, Duleep and his legendary uncle, Ranji, were heroes of style and grace made all the more romantic by their origins and birth. Admiration for others is all very well but not to be taken too seriously and much better indulged in from a distance. I find it is usually a mistake to meet one's heroes as it invariably leads to disappointment. So we have no problem here with Duleep, whose life can be quietly absorbed like a good novel in which the reader can use his imagination to conjure up the character and essence of the man.

Duleep's life was plagued by ill-health and it was a deep sadness to his many supporters and friends when his cricketing career was cut short by illness when he was only 27 years old in 1932. For so long he had been laid low by tuberculosis which at times severely restricted his capacity to display his extraordinary talent. All the same, Sussex came so close to winning the County Championship in his final year and, indeed, might have done so had not Duleep collapsed at Taunton in August, never to play again. Concealed beneath the veneer of elegance and style there lay the scourge of an illness for which doctors had yet to find a cure.

This book, amongst much else, will inspire the reader to wonder what might have been. After all, Duleep was cruelly thwarted in the prime of his cricketing life. Surely his international career would have continued to flourish and perhaps in the 1930s Sussex might have won the County Championship, so often the preserve of Yorkshire. As it was, his county had to wait another 71 years to reach this coveted landmark.

Duleep's powers of leadership would certainly have developed more fully. It seemed that the pressures of captaincy weighed heavily upon him both physically and emotionally. He is described in the book as "inspirational and unobtrusive" and, at Cheltenham College, the school to which he came from India to attend, as "a player of both brains and brilliance". Duleep had more or less everything running his way except his health.

On a different note, but none the less interesting, it appears that Duleep bowled very little in first class cricket, preferring to stand at slip where he reigned supreme and became one of the most outstanding catchers in the country. And yet at Cheltenham in his teens he was an extremely promising leg-spinner who apparently deceived batsmen with very slow deliveries or lobs - and spun the ball viciously. There have been plenty of precocious leg-spinners the world over but, as they grow and their fingers fatten, they mostly fall by the wayside and lose their creative talent. The disease has become known for some reason as the "yips" and there have been many sufferers over the years. I wonder what happened to Duleep and his slow bowling?

Duleep has now been dead for over 45 years and last played cricket some 70 years ago. And yet this book has brought a charming cricketer and servant of the game back to life with a richness of spirit which will be compelling for its readers. Sussex members in their deckchairs at Hove, no longer Eastbourne and Hastings, sadly, will enjoy hearing about the thrashing Duleep dished out to Tich Freeman. And not only Sussex people, but cricket enthusiasts everywhere, will be fascinated to read about Duleep and his contribution to the game's history.

Few have been more successful than Duleep in such a short time. In his calm and composed way he never struck me as a greedy player but he did like scoring runs. Don't we all! The secret of his game lay in its artistry. Perhaps he came close to creating his own golden age to reflect something of his uncle's era and that of his guardian in England, C.B.Fry.

Duleep showed charm and courtesy, which was never more evident than in the diplomatic and administrative world in which he moved after cricket. He was modest and humble and showed unassuming integrity and strength of character. And yet he was surely no saint. There were suggestions of arrogance, but how hard it is to tell the difference between this unattractive trait and the supreme confidence of one who played with such majesty. As Chairman of the Indian selectors, and later as a journalist, it was not always easy to keep everyone happy. Nor did he. Neither task went hand in hand with the gentle world for which Duleep was more associated.

Duleep, without doubt, brought sunshine into the lives of many. His talent was sandwiched between two World Wars and did much to lighten the darkness which was, within a few years, to threaten the world. And what a great draw he was, an attractive figure and an unfashionable one, too, in his time. Indians were then rarely seen in the field in England and had yet to play in Test cricket.

Barry Rickson has given us a fine book to savour in which his perception matches Duleep's speed of eye and foot. It will remind us of the chivalry and joy of an age not far gone but which did much to shape the nature of the modern game.

1.

A SEASON OF TRIUMPH AND TRAGEDY

Sussex County Cricket Club 1932

KUMAR SHRI DULEEPSINHJI, known to everybody as Duleep, had been spending the winter of 1931/32 in his native India when he received the invitation from the Sussex Secretary to captain the county again after his successful leadership in the previous season. Sussex had risen three places to fourth in the County Championship with his captaincy gaining "golden opinions". He had taken over after the side had been led for several years by the Gilligan brothers AER and AHH, fine cricketers both of whom had led their country. They were a hard act to follow, but Duleep's charm, modesty, chivalrous manner and personal skills as a great cricketer had made the transition a smooth one.

There was quiet optimism at Hove that the northern stranglehold of Lancashire and Yorkshire could be realistically challenged. *The Cricketer* magazine in its issue of May 7 stated that with all the young players they had Sussex were almost certain to improve. They had a fine squad with strength in all departments. The captain himself was one of the best two or three batsmen in the country and he was supported by such stalwarts as England player Ted Bowley, Harry Parks, his up-and-coming brother Jim, ex-England soccer centre-forward Tom Cook and the very promising John Langridge. For all-rounders Duleep could call upon cricketers such as the great Maurice Tate, still one of the finest bowlers in England, and the elder Langridge, James, a left-arm spin bowler and rapidly improving batsman, whilst Bowley was a very useful bowler. Spearheading the attack with Tate was the indefatigable Bert Wensley, also a good enough batsman to score 1,000 runs in a season four times and do the "Double" in 1929. The wicketkeeper was "Tich" Cornford, who had played with Duleep and Bowley for England on the 1929/30 tour of New Zealand, and the overall youthfulness of the side ensured that the fielding would be keen and athletic; moreover, once the University match was completed they would be strengthened by the addition of the very promising Oxford batsman from South Africa, Alan Melville, and now fully available was Wykehamist and Oxford Blue RSG Scott, fast-medium bowler and hard-hitting late-order batsman.

With such a talented side Duleep and the club's players, committee and supporters started the season in good heart. He would not be called upon for Test cricket as there was to be only one Test that season, the first-ever between England and India. He did not wish to offend the susceptibilities of his countrymen by playing against them, particularly as he had turned down the chance of being their captain!

The only cloud on the horizon would seem to be continuing doubts about his health as he was never completely clear of the problems of pulmonary tuberculosis which had first started to affect his cricket early in the 1927 season. After a wonderful start he had been compelled to give up playing in early May and did not play again until the end of May 1928 having spent the winter in a sanatorium in Switzerland.

Ironically the first match of the season for Sussex was against the tourists who made an excellent impression considering their unfamiliarity with English conditions. Duleep himself was dismissed for a mere seven. Although he made several useful scores, such as 74 against Middlesex at Lord's, 60 at Leicester, when he also made several "clever catches", 62 in the return game at Hastings and 89 versus Gloucestershire at Horsham, he did not really come into his own until the second match in the Horsham week when his 116 was an important factor in Sussex's win by an innings and 102 runs. His "well-varied strokes" were the feature of his two-and-three-quarter-hour innings. At this stage the county had won four championship matches, three by an innings, and had also beaten Cambridge University by the same margin. Unfortunately in this match against his alma mater he was dismissed for nought, the future West Indies captain Rolph Grant catching him smartly off the bowling of RC Rought-Rought. The 74 at Lord's was made in the benefit match for that great Middlesex player Jack Hearne but the Whitsun fixture was ruined by rain. His score was by far the highest in what play there was, each side completing an innings, with his efforts being described as "most skilful batting".

A week after the Worcestershire match Surrey came to Hove in a non-championship game when both sides turned out their best teams with the exception of Jack Hobbs for the visitors. Sussex carried on their winning ways with yet another innings victory after scoring 536. Duleep's share was 126, an innings described by *Wisden* thus: "Batting with delightful finesse and exploiting practically every stroke in most skilful fashion, Duleepsinhji played absolutely faultless cricket." Whilst his county were occupied in the return fixture at Hove with Cambridge University, Duleep travelled to Old Trafford for the Test trial, representing the South against the North. In what must have been a connoisseur's delight, Duleep, playing "in masterly fashion", added 174 in two hours with Walter Hammond. His cutting and leg-glancing were as elegant as always and added to this was driving of great power. His only chance came when Larwood's attempt at a caught-and-bowled from a ferocious return drive was rewarded with a badly damaged hand! He was eventually dismissed in this manner when Larwood's great partner, Bill Voce, held on to what was presumably not quite so hot a chance.

Returning to county duty for Sussex at Headingley he spent a long time in the field as Yorkshire scored 500 for 8 declared. Herbert Sutcliffe's 270 brought his aggregate for his last four innings up to 789, including what was to be the highest score of his career, 313 against Essex in a partnership of 555 with Percy Holmes which was to stand as a world record for almost forty-five years. Practically unnoticed it seems amidst all this run-riot was a wonderful analysis of 7-99 in thirty-seven overs by Jim Parks. Although Sussex were forced to follow on 241 runs behind, they saved the game with ease. In their first innings there were only two innings of substance, Ted Bowley scoring 90 before being run out, and Duleep, who "drove particularly well", 83. In the follow-on Duleep's 91 before falling to the wiles of Hedley Verity ensured a draw for Sussex. He received substantial assistance from Tom Cook with 67 in a partnership of 126, batting without error.

From Headingley Sussex travelled south to Edgbaston where Duleep scored only 18 but he would not have been too disappointed as his team had yet another innings victory, this time over Warwickshire. The heroes were Bowley 162 and Cook 160 with the bat and James Langridge 9- 124 in the match and Wensley 6-73 in the second innings with the ball. Returning northwards, the next port of call was Old Trafford. The game with Lancashire at the end of June was rain-affected so that neither side was able to gain any clear advantage. Lancashire's score of 413 was dominated by a county record sixth-wicket stand of 278, a record which still stands, by Jack Iddon and HRW Butterworth. Iddon's 201 was one of several double centuries he made for the county, but his partner, a Cambridge Blue of 1929, made his only first-class century in scoring 107. In reply Sussex scored 322 for 5 with Duleep batting "in delightful form" to score 111 in just over two and a half-hours.

Sussex then had a wonderful run of four games in which they beat Glamorgan and Northants by an innings, Kent by ten wickets and Worcestershire by nine. Duleep himself did very little with the bat in three of these matches, but whilst his county were defeating Northants he managed to score what was to be the last century of his career for the Gentlemen against the Players in the Lord's match. Facing a Players' total of 301 which contained an innings of 110 by Walter Hammond at his most majestic, the Gentlemen replied with 430 for 8 declared. The highlight of the innings was a partnership of 161 between the two Indians, Duleep and the Nawab of Pataudi. As *The Times* of July 15 reported, "Of the two KS Duleepsinhji was the more exuberant... Each, in fact, played his part superbly for his side, and if the Nawab of Pataudi is the more generously rewarded by the score card, it was KS Duleepsinhji who made such great things possible." Duleep was finally dismissed for 132, whilst Pataudi went on to score 165. Duleep was careful to play himself in but after two narrow escapes batted in his best form. The Players' bowling was high-class with an attack consisting of Larwood, Voce, Tate, Freeman, Hammond and Woolley. Even so, it was reported that "the Players could never have seen a glimmer of hope while KS Duleepsinhji and the Nawab of Pataudi remained together." Duleep, against his old adversary "Tich" Freeman, played him "exquisitely, with a quick step down the pitch and his bat perfectly straight to the flight of the ball. Voce he cut or put away to leg with a short-armed hook, and when Hammond came on he gave us the pleasure of the straight drive which hit the sight screen first bounce, or was yards too fast for an out fieldsman to gather." The Indian tourists read of this game with mixed feelings as they would dearly have loved one or both of them to have been in their side for the previous month's Test with England at Lord's. Pataudi's innings was described in *The Cricketer* as "truly magnificent".

Duleep scored but twelve runs in total in three innings in his county's next two games against Kent at Maidstone and Lancashire at Hove. That prolific wicket-taker "Tich" Freeman claimed him as one of his 253 victims of the season when he bowled him for 8 in a match which Sussex won yet again, this time by 10 wickets, whilst at Hove Frank Sibbles dismissed him for 3 and 1 in a drawn game. Sibbles was a fine medium-pace bowler who took just under one thousand wickets for his county in a career stretching from 1925 to 1937 and later served as a committee man in the post-war years. After 35 against Essex at Clacton, Duleep played in a further Test Trial at Cardiff in which rain allowed only less than three hours' play in total. In what play was possible Duleep showed to great advantage in an innings of 92*. "The spectators in seeing Duleepsinhji at his best had some reward for their patience."

Whilst Duleep was engaged in this match, his county were also playing in a rain-affected match with Derbyshire at Hove which finished in an inconclusive draw but not before Harry Parks had scored 150* for the home side and the future South African captain Alan Melville had marked his debut with an elegant 52. Returning to the county side at

Hove, Duleep led his men to yet another innings victory, this time against Middlesex. His contribution with the bat was a mere 29, the hero of the team being the splendid Maurice Tate whose 50 at number 10, the second highest score, was followed by bowling figures of 7-28 and 6-30.

There were signs, however, that the strains of leadership and the chase for the championship were beginning to take their toll. His health was also causing great concern with the returning symptoms of the enervating pulmonary tuberculosis becoming more and more apparent as the summer progressed. Although one cannot lay all the blame for his inconsistency at the door of ill-health, it must have been a contributory factor in the run of poor scores at this stage of the season.

A six-wicket victory over Northants at Hastings in a low-scoring game with Duleep scoring 31 and 15 was followed by a double failure for him against Kent at Hastings. At the same ground against the same opponents in 1929 he had enjoyed one of the greatest triumphs of his career with 115 and 246; this time he only managed 4 and 0 in a drawn game.

What an anti-climactic ending for what was to prove to be his final home game for the county! At this stage with seven matches to play Sussex were lying second in the table to Yorkshire and with one game in hand were only nineteen points behind. As there were fifteen points to be awarded for an outright win and Yorkshire were to come to Hove at the end of August, the situation was becoming very interesting. Lancashire were no longer a threat as they were seventy points behind at this stage. Kent were six points behind Duleep's side, but they had played two games more. The only other realistic challengers were perhaps Nottinghamshire, thirty-five points behind Yorkshire having played the same number of games.

At the end of the Gentlemen versus Players match in mid-July the MCC released the names of the first five players selected to go on the tour to Australia and New Zealand. The selection of this side was a rather long drawn-out affair with different groups being chosen until the team was finally completed in late August. In the first group - Douglas Jardine had already been selected as captain - were Herbert Sutcliffe, Walter Hammond, Duleepsinhji, Les Ames and George Duckworth; in other words the two wicketkeepers and the three major batsmen. Duleep's position in English cricket could not have been made more evident.

After the Kent encounter Sussex moved on to Swansea to play Glamorgan. Yet again they won by an innings even though batting first they scored only 272. At last Duleep found some form for his county, as after a disheartening sequence of a mere 126 runs in his previous nine innings he made 83 which was twice as high as the next highest score in the match. He started nervously but settled down to play almost at his best with his usual array of shots, his cutting particularly catching the eye. *The Times* announced his innings as "Duleepsinhji's return to form" and commented how after an uncertain opening he recovered and "after luncheon hit with delightful freedom all round the wicket", However, when he seemed to have the bowling mastered, he gave a tame catch to short-leg. Could this have been further evidence of his illness and general lack of strength? James Langridge and Bert Wensley with match figures of 9-65 and 8-91 respectively bowled out the home side for 96 and 134.

However, Duleep's health was now causing great concern and his doctors strongly advised him not to play on. Uncle Ranji, hearing of his nephew's loss of form and thrilled at his old county's championship prospects, contacted him from the distant Aix-les-Bains. Unfortunately, he had not realised the seriousness of Duleep's situation and told his nephew that he must continue. The cable was mostly encouraging but contained the words: "Think more of the interests of your side than of your reputation," which seems rather like some sort of moral blackmail. He finished by saying that he put Duleep's fielding above most people's batting, " ....Therefore go on. Love and Success." Duleep was in awe of his uncle and this message was treated as a royal command. Rather unwisely, therefore, he failed to heed the advice of his doctors and went on from Swansea to play at Taunton against Somerset. Sussex gained yet another convincing victory, this time by ten wickets with Duleep's 90 being the highest score of the match. He took part in a stand of 148 in just over two hours with James Langridge showing "delightful form". In one period of fifteen minutes he added thirty runs while his partner made four. The physical cost, however, was enormous and he batted in increasing distress, being exhausted and haemorrhaging. He never again set foot as a player on a cricket field and thus ended the career of a truly great cricketer at the tragically young age of 27. The Australian cricketer turned writer, RS Whitington, was of the opinion that Duleep "would probably have lived many more years, had he not put cricket even ahead of life on that autumn day in 1932".

There were hopes that he may return before the end of the season to lead his county's challenge to Yorkshire, but it was not to be. *The Times* reported that he would be taking a week's rest as he was suffering from an attack of sciatica and arthritis, but hoped to be available to lead Sussex against Yorkshire and Somerset during the Hove Cricket Week. Little did they realise the seriousness of Duleep's illness. Intriguingly, he was selected to play in the Scarborough Festival against the Indian tourists for HDG Leveson Gower's XI in a strong side containing those such as Hobbs, Sutcliffe, Leyland and Hendren. How interesting it would have been if he had made a big score against his fellow-countrymen, having declined to play for them in their Test baptism!

Ironically, Sussex's next match after the Somerset game at Taunton was at Cheltenham College, his old school, where Sussex kept up their challenge with a 56 run victory over Gloucestershire. Charlie Parker and Tom Goddard set their usual problems for the home side but they were "outspun" by James Langridge with wonderful figures of 7-8 and 6-59. This was to prove to be Sussex's last win of the season. The eagerly awaited game with Yorkshire at Hove at the end of August proved to be an easy victory by 167 runs for the northerners against a Sussex side not only without Duleep, but also such key players as Ted Bowley and Bert Wensley who were both injured. Sutcliffe scored an inevitable century, Bill Bowes took eight wickets in the first innings, twelve in the match, and Hedley Verity six in the second innings. For Sussex the only real performance of note was Maurice Tate's 6-79 in the first innings.

Sussex did manage to finish runners-up but the final margin was fifty-three points. Yorkshire had enjoyed a most impressive end of season with nine consecutive wins and would more than likely have won the title in any event, but it is one of those intriguing questions that can never be answered - just how much were Sussex affected by the loss of Duleep's batting skills and inspirational leadership?

He finished the season at Taunton with 1,633 runs at an average of 52.67 and headed his county's averages with 1139 runs at 45.56 with a clear lead of over six runs from Harry Parks. All these are very respectable figures, but of his five centuries only two were scored in the County Championship as he reserved his best form for other games. That Sussex won so many games by an innings was, of course, an important reason for scoring fewer runs than in previous seasons but for the first time his overall season's average was higher than that for his county. Was the strain of the high expectations at the start of the season for Sussex's title hopes a contributory factor in hastening on the return of his dreaded illness? Did he feel that the dual responsibilities of being leading batsman and captain had become a little too much? Had the question of his split loyalties to England and the emerging India Test team had any effect on his peace of mind?

The fact is, however, that Sussex had a marvellous season under his captaincy. Of their fourteen victories eight were won by an innings, two by ten wickets and one by nine wickets. They had dismissed their opponents for under one hundred ten times in championship games, their own lowest score being 133 at Cheltenham against Gloucestershire and even then they won the game comfortably. Their only loss of the season came in the penultimate match with Yorkshire.

Sussex were hoping that he would be able to resume the captaincy the following season, but in spite of further treatment in a sanatorium in Switzerland he felt compelled to resign the captaincy of the county with the scarcely reassuring conclusion that "I am afraid that my playing days are over for at least five years." Ranji was, of course, filled with remorse when he discovered the true situation of his nephew's condition, bitterly regretting the telegraph he had sent him on the eve of the Somerset match when he was not fully au fait with the circumstances.

As we have seen, Duleep was one of the first choices for the tour to Australia, but on medical advice, which he heeded this time, was forced to withdraw. His uncle, still feeling very guilty about his earlier message, sent him another telegram to try to overcome his great disappointment: "Do not get depressed." He went on to say that the doctor in charge of the case and his assistants would do all in their power to cure him. Duleep "must assist them with your will power and cheeriness". Ranji would send him to Australia as soon as he was well. He concluded: "Cheer up. My love and sympathy. You have had remarkable success this year and are sure to do better later."

The Times of 1 September noted that E Paynter of Lancashire had been selected to take part in the MCC tour and KS Duleepsinhji would not be able to sail with the rest of the side on September 17, but it was hoped that he would be able to join the team later. What a tragically vain hope that was!

There was great sympathy shown to him by the whole of the cricketing world, these sentiments being lucidly expressed by MA Tanfield in *The Cricketer* of 17 September 1932. "Cricketers all over the world will stretch out their hands in sympathy to KS Duleepsinhji in his illness which prevents him going to Australia. His loss to the team is not to be measured - and he will be missed not only on the field but off it - for his charm of manner, his great modesty, and his nicely balanced mentality have endeared him to all who have had the pleasure of meeting him. He will be ever in the thoughts of those who should have been his colleagues. May he speedily recover his health and strength and be his own great self when next season comes round."

Wisden was moved to write a glowing tribute to him in the following terms:

One of the ablest cricketers and one of the most charming of men, after all too brief a sojourn amongst us, there passed from the game he had adorned with such conspicuous grace and success, one of the most beautiful batsmen of recent years. English cricket in general and that of Sussex in particular will be all the poorer for his enforced absence. A young man of singular charm and character; extremely modest of his own wonderful ability; and with a love of the game which transcended his joy in all other pastimes, Duleepsinhji will always be remembered as one of the outstanding personalities during his period in first-class cricket.

The minutes of the General Committee of the county of September 30, 1932 note: "KS Duleepsinhji - The Secretary was deputed to write a letter to KS Duleepsinhji, sympathising with him on his being unable to join the England Team to Australia, owing to his serious illness." It goes on to thank RSG Scott for his great services to the club during the past season before recording that the Secretary had been given permission to follow the beagles on Tuesdays and Saturdays during the winter months!

The New Zealand cricketing authorities expressed their sympathy as they had been so looking forward to his return after his memorable visit to them with the MCC in 1929/30.

On the eve of the team's sailing to Australia he was sent a telegram from Pelham Warner on behalf of himself and his fellow joint Manager, Richard Palairet, Douglas Jardine and the rest of the side. His inability to make the trip would be regretted as much by the Australians as by his team-mates, and Warner concluded: "We send you best wishes,

31

speedy recovery. We shall miss you greatly on and off the field."

On September 28 W Findlay, the Secretary of the MCC, sent him a letter to Jamnagar House, Staines, Middlesex, expressing his great regret at Duleep's inability to travel with the side and offered to come and see him if he so wished. "I do feel so desperately sorry about it all."

Perhaps the most moving tribute to him was the letter sent to him in mid-September by Douglas Jardine from aboard the boat to Australia. Jardine has the image in many quarters of being a remote, unsmiling, unfeeling martinet with little sensitivity towards most of his fellow men - certainly the Australians thought this after his visit there with APF Chapman's side in 1928/29, a feeling strongly reinforced at the end of the forthcoming Test series, one to be forever known as the summer of "Bodyline"! An early indication of the other side of his character appears in this letter.

How very nice of you to write to me, though I wish you had not exerted yourself to do so. Thank you for your charming letter.

I haven't written since I went up to Scotland for fear of worrying you, but now I can only say that with the exception of yourself, there is none more sadly disappointed at your tragic bad luck than myself.

I know I could count on you and looked forward so much to your help and advice in our difficult task - believe me I do not forget how you have gone out of your way to be helpful to me to my face and behind my back (sic). I am very

grateful - but apart from all that, Duleep, I like
you so much and value your friendship so much
that I can only hold out my hand to you in silent
sympathy, while also sympathising with myself
on losing the right hand man of the team... Take
care of yourself and let me know how you get on.

What greater testimony could one have of the
popularity and beautiful character of Duleep than
this moving and emotional letter from a man held
to be so lacking in feeling? To put the record
straight, it must be said that Jardine gained great
respect and admiration from his men (with the
possible exceptions of the Nawab of Pataudi and
"Gubby" Allen) as for example Hedley Verity who,
when his son was born in June 1933 in the middle
of a "Roses" match at Old Trafford, named him
Douglas.

Let us now trace the steps of his cricketing days
which led to this sad ending after such a glorious
career. It is a journey which will take us from
Rajkumar College in Rajkot, a school for those from
privileged families in the north-west of India, to the
county grounds of England. It is a journey which
will take in Cheltenham College in Gloucestershire,
Clare College at Cambridge University, Australia,
New Zealand and most of England's homes of first-
class and Test cricket, mainly on behalf of Sussex
County Cricket Club.

2.

EARLY DAYS AND
CHELTENHAM COLLEGE

KUMAR SHRI DULEEPSINHJI was born into a princely family in the state of Nawanagar on June 13, 1905. His father was the younger brother of the great cricketer Kumar Shri Ranjitsinhji who in 1907 became the Jam Saheb of Nawanagar. Following in the footsteps of his three elder brothers he was sent to a boarding school in July 1914, the prestigious Rajkumar College at Rajkot, alma mater of the great statesman Gandhi. This was one of four schools set up by the Government of India in order to "fit the young Chiefs and Nobles of India physically, morally and intellectually for the responsibilities that lay before them" with the idea that instead of being "solitary suns in petty firmaments" they would become "co-ordinate atoms in a larger whole". In 1870 the college, in the centre of the Kathiawar peninsula, was the first of the four to be set up. Duleep, in his turn, also eventually had cricketing nephews. Hanumant Singh, who became the Maharajkumar of Banswara, represented India in fourteen Tests, including a tour of England in 1967, whilst KS Indrajitsinhji kept wicket for his country in four Tests in the 1960s.

He had received much coaching and encouragement from his uncle and his talent was perceived at an early stage when he scored a century at the age of 13 in a match in which all the best cricketers in the school took part. He was successful not only on the games field, but also in the classroom, as he won the Diamond Jubilee Prize for being top of his class on four occasions. In addition, his courteous disposition and charm, lifelong attributes, had already made their impact on all who knew him.

In April 1919 it was decided to further his education by sending him to England to study at St. Faith's, a preparatory school in Cambridge under the headship of the distinguished RS Goodchild. The school had been recommended by Uncle Ranji who had strong connections there. His cricketing ability made an immediate impact causing Mr Goodchild to comment that at the wicket he was "invincible".

By this time Ranjitsinhji was having more and more influence on his nephew's upbringing, as well as supporting him financially, and chose as his public school Malvern in Worcestershire. He was unable to gain entry as there was an unusually high intake of boys that year, so it was decided that he should go to the nearby Cheltenham College in Gloucestershire. The fact that his elder brother - in later life to be Major-General Himatsinhji - was already a student at Malvern caused much friendly family rivalry over the years as to the respective merits of the two colleges. Consequently, he entered Cheltenham as a 14-year-old in January 1920 together with his cousin Kumar Shri Ramsinhji. It is a surprising fact that all of the college's records, beginning with the details on his application form completed on October 18, 1919, show as his date of birth June 20, 1906, rather than the correct one stated previously. It was during his years at Cheltenham, 1920-23, that the wider cricketing world began to take notice.

Cheltenham College, a most prestigious public school in a very attractive part of the county, opened at its present site on Bath Road in 1843. It is known amongst other things for its beautiful chapel, its strong connection with preparing boys for Sandhurst and Woolwich from about 1860 until 1960, and for its first-class cricket ground where each season the Cheltenham Festival takes place with Gloucestershire County Cricket Club playing host to at least two other leading counties. In such a setting Duleep would thrive. In his time there the school had approximately 541 students, all boys, with 456 boarders and 85 day boys. The college went fully co-educational in September 1998 with the present numbers being 396 boys and 183 girls. As is to be expected, there have been many pupils who went on to achieve great fame or distinction. Before Duleep's time there were the Antarctic explorer Dr. Edward Wilson, who died with Scott, Lord Morley, a member of Lloyd George's government, and the Renshaw twins, Willie and Ernest, who monopolised men's tennis in the 1880s. More or less contemporary to Duleep were the writers Patrick White and John Masters; the former, an Australian, won the Nobel Prize as a novelist for *The Eye of the Storm*, whilst the latter achieved fame with his Indian-based stories, such as *Bhowani Junction* and *The Road Past Mandalay*. In more recent times the college has produced politicians such as the Deputy Speaker Alan Haselhurst, Ivor Richard, Ambassador to the USA, soldiers of the calibre of General Sir Michael Rose, United Nations leader in Bosnia, one of fifty-three major-generals and above or equivalents in the Royal Navy or Royal Air Force, and the great squash player Jonah Barrington. The strong military element can be seen in the award of 14 VCs to Old Boys in battles raging from Afghanistan to Zanzibar. One of the more memorable events in the Iraq war was the toppling of the statue of Saddam Hussein which was reported on TV by BBC journalist, Old Cheltonian Rageh Omaar. To bring us right up until the present day we also have the Chief Executive of Kent County Cricket Club and first-class squash player Paul Millman. Duleep obviously takes his place amongst this distinguished group.

His guardian was named as his ex-headmaster Mr RS Goodchild, whilst his tutor at St. Faith's, Mr H Lower, when asked as to what was his likely career, suggested for Duleep and his cousin "Engineer, as far as we can tell," which hardly seems too decisive an opinion. In fact he was placed in the "Classical and Modern" side rather than the "Military and Engineering" and was a member of the Day Boys' house. He stayed with Montague Seaton in his house Muttrapore in Sandy Lane. His first term's work in 2 Modern was most promising with his form teacher's report summing up his efforts as "Excellent, I like the way he shapes." In this term he had performed most creditably in Maths. where he was placed in Set 1. "Thoroughly good progress" was recorded in 3 Modern.

In the middle years of his school career he was rewarded with the Div. Maths. Prize, but there were indications that he was having difficulties with the language side. "Good work but handicapped by expression", "Works well but handicapped by English", and "Suffers from lack of English idiom" were some of the comments on his reports, whilst it was felt that having to study four languages was very difficult for him. Although generally placed in lower sets for these subjects, he impressed his teachers with his efforts and his ability in Maths - always in the top sets - enabled him to finish in respectable form positions overall. In fact in 4 Modern he finished top in his German set of 18 and had made a considerable improvement in his French position. His English Literature class texts were as one would expect from a school such as Cheltenham in that period with a very heavy emphasis on Shakespeare and Tennyson, supplemented by works not too familiar in more recent times, such as Robert Louis Stevenson's set of essays *Virginibus Puerisque* and AW Kinglake's *Eothen*, a book considered to be a classic work on travel.

As we have seen, Duleep's personality was such as to charm all who knew him and this, allied to his hard-working conscientious nature, made it natural that he should become a House and then College Prefect. In this latter capacity his signature together with those of the other prefects may be seen on a form in the school archives sanctioning the punishment of six strokes of the cane as ordered by the Senior Prefect, one CFE Harvey, to two boys. The two boys were not where they should have been and four prefects were given the task of administering justice.

So much for Duleepsinhji the scholar, but what about his distinguished sporting career at the College? Although he had come to the school with something of a reputation as a cricketer and as the nephew of the great Ranjitsinhji, he had to serve an apprenticeship, as it were, and began by playing for his House 2nd XI in 1920. He graduated rapidly to the House 1st XI through to the school Colts XI and played twice for the school XXII or 2nd XI. In one of his games for the Colts against keen rivals Malvern, for whom he had failed to gain entrance in 1919, he scored 149* out of a total of 222, his score being the exact total of Malvern's reply. The captain of Malvern told him several years later that he realised then that Duleepsinhji would one day play for England. His two appearances on the 2nd XI were rewarded with the highest score on each occasion. It was during this period that he came under the influence of the ex-Gloucestershire player Billy Woof who as coach at the school did so much to help set him on the right path and to whom Duleep was eternally grateful.

It was obvious that 1921 would see him as a key player in the 1st XI and the school magazine, *The Cheltonian*, of May 21 carried extracts from an article in *The Morning Post* when no less an authority than PF Warner commented that "A nephew of the Jam of Nawanagar (Ranji) played well as a colt last year when he scored a hundred against Malvern Colts and should obtain a place in the side."

This is obviously what happened, but what is perhaps surprising is that his bowling was just as effective as his batting. In the match with deadly rivals Marlborough he was brought on to bowl when they seemed to be on the verge of a large score but his well tossed-up slow leg-breaks caused havoc. A potentially large total became an all-out one of 166 with Duleep taking 7-35. When Cheltenham went in to bat he scored 76 out of a total of 399 for 9 dec. His cutting was deemed to have been especially good with his tendency in his early years to be a stronger leg-side player also discernible. His school won the match by an innings and 103 runs with his slip-fielding also being prominent. Hardly surprisingly he was given his school 1st XI colours after the game. Against the Old Cheltonians his 7-64 was some consolation for "failing to trouble the scorers", but in the MCC match he was successful with bat and ball scoring 56 and taking four wickets; this was a significant contribution to the college's first victory over the MCC for many years. At the climax of the season his bowling skills were again revealed with his 6-76 against Clifton CC as well as top score in the match of 51 in a 20 run victory.

The Cheltonian's comments on his perform-ances were: "A good all-round cricketer. With more power will score more easily in front of the wicket. Has a good late-cut through slips, but too often fell a victim to a catch at the wicket or in the slips. A good slip-fielder and bowler." He finished the season third in batting (279 runs at an average of 31.1) and bowling (most wickets 39 at 17.13). The 16-year-old could feel very pleased with his start.

The May 1922 edition of *The Cricketer* noted that given his family background a great deal would be expected of Duleepsinhji who had shown such exceptional form for a boy of his age the previous summer. "Duleepsinhji will not be 16 until the end of July (in fact it would be mid-June when he would be 17) but one of the finest judges of the game in England who has seen a good deal of his cricket thinks that he will make almost as great a name for himself as his famous uncle."

Before the beginning of the next cricket season it was noted in *The Times* Public School Sports section that on Friday, March 31, in "very unfavourable weather" (What do they expect if they hold athletics events then?), KS Duleepsinhji had won the Under-16 Long Jump with a leap of 17ft 1in.

Now an established member of the XI for the 1922 season, Duleep started rather disappointingly with the bat with a "duck" against Cheltenham Town and 4 against the Gloucester Gypsies. In this match he did, however, take 7-75 and could enjoy a remarkable display of hitting by his colleague, CJ King-Turner, who scored 187* with twenty-six fours and seven sixes. Against Liverpool CC he also failed with the bat, scoring only 1, but more than made amends with his leg-breaks with figures of 8-60. In the match with the Old Cheltonians he "played excellent cricket" for his 52, but continued to shine more with the ball. Against Clifton he took 11-72 in the match followed by 6-22 against Clifton Town. In the annual match at Lord's, Cheltenham v Haileybury, there was extensive coverage in *The Times* for a contest which had a thrilling end with Cheltenham finishing just four runs behind with six wickets in hand. Duleep finished with 76* after a first-innings failure and there were many allusions to the potential danger presented by his bowling, as although he took only two wickets in the second innings, he beat the bat repeatedly.

He was selected to play at Lord's in the match immediately following this for The Lord's Schools v The Rest. It is interesting to note that also selected for the side was Lord Dunglass from Eton, who as Sir Alec Douglas-Home became Conservative Prime Minister in 1963-64 for 366 days. The twelfth men for each side became distinguished players. For the Lord's Schools EW Dawson of Eton played for England five times, captained Cambridge University in 1927 and Leicestershire for four seasons; for The Rest ERT Holmes of Malvern also played for England five times, captained Oxford University, again in 1927, thus opposing Dawson in the Varsity match, and Surrey for seven seasons.

Although he did not distinguish himself with the bat on this occasion, his fielding was remarked upon in a newspaper report: ".....Duleepsinhji made a very fine catch at short-leg which got rid of JV Richardson. Duleepsinhji anticipated the flight of the ball a good yard and made another pace to the left to hold it down with both hands."

Incidentally, the future Prime Minister took 3-22 in eleven overs in the only innings of The Rest after scoring 14.

Duleep again finished third in the batting averages with 264 runs at an average of 26.4, but comfortably headed the bowling with 50 wickets - next best 32 - at 13.66. For their efforts in the season the captain ALS Jackson, the afore-mentioned King-Turner and Duleep were awarded Troughton Memorial bats.

The Cheltonian noted that he was a good all-round cricketer, but only found his true batting form on two occasions.

The Cricketer commented that he had not developed as a batsman quite as much as had been anticipated but "of his potentiality there can be little question; perhaps he has not yet mastered the grammar of defence". His 50 wickets with his slow leg-breaks were duly noted.

In 1923, to nobody's surprise, Duleep was made captain. The now defunct *Ayres Cricket Companion* described him as "A first-rate bat, useful bowler and splendid field", and, rather enigmatically, "...he was no square peg in a round hole". The May 1923 edition of *The Cricketer*, in its notes on Cheltenham College for the season, commented that, "On his day the captain himself is capable of going through a side with his slow spin bowling. Already he is said to possess a sound knowledge of the game, but then cricket is in his blood, for is he not a relative of the great

Ranji himself?" A rare feature of his game, which would be commented on repeatedly in his first-class days, was already apparent at Cheltenham, namely, his ability to take stunning one-handed slip catches. It had been forecast at the beginning of the season that "Duleepsinhji should make runs in plenty" and so it proved. Early in the season against Cheltenham Town he scored 103 out of 176 for 6 declared with "One and a half hours of faultless and most graceful cricket". His 78 against Marlborough in a ten-wicket victory, together with six wickets in the match, was followed shortly by his highest ever score for the school of 162 in the annual encounter with the Old Boys. He reached his century in just under two hours, "scoring freely all round the wicket". His bowling was still a vital element as in just under 250 overs he took 35 wickets at 18.40 each, with 5-34 against Marlborough and 7-37 in the Clifton CC match being his best returns. With the bat he had his best season for the school with 576 runs at 52.36 which led to an invitation to play once more for the Lord's Schools v The Rest. He caught the eye with a magnificent innings of 108 at a run a minute, " making beautiful strokes all round the wicket with delightful ease". In the Rest's follow-on he shone with the ball, taking 5-41. "He did not appear at all enterprising but runs flowed from his bat with almost monotonous regularity... Those whipcord wrists turned the ball in all directions.... an innings of graceful batting allied to superlative application."

His form in this game led to his selection for the Public Schools' XI against the Army when in a short innings of 25 he gave further evidence of his class. He made some "grand strokes" said *The Times* and although "Probably, almost certainly, he will never be able to play such an innings as did the Jam Sahib in 1896 at Manchester against Australia" (a reference to Ranjitsinhji's 154* on his Test debut) the writer goes on to say that "almost anything else is within his possibilities". *The Cheltonian* saw him as "a thoroughly good captain with a sound knowledge of the game. Set a splendid example both on and off the field. A first-rate bat, useful bowler and beautiful field."

Several years later Duleep gave great credit for his success to his coach at school, the ex-Gloucestershire professional, William Albert Woof. "All I know about the game, all the successes I have gained, all those to come my way in the future, I owe to one man - Old Woofy."

HS Altham, a most respected judge of the game, in his notes of the 1923 Public School season held him to be the player of the season, commenting particularly on his "natural gifts of eye, wrist and footwork". His batting had made great strides forward, whilst "his defence has gained markedly in correctness and self-control... his range of scoring shots is altogether exceptional for a school batsman". Of particular note were his beautiful late cutting, powerful, orthodox driving and ability to turn straight balls square of mid-on for runs. Altham further noted that his fielding, especially at slip, was first-class. Great interest would be taken in his future when he could also become a most useful bowler.

During his school holidays he had kept himself in practice by playing for the legendary CB Fry's Training ship Mercury. An astute judge of a cricketer, he considered the young Duleep to be by far the best for his age he had seen. Duleep also made an appearance for the Indian Gymkhana at Lord's v the MCC. He performed most creditably with 48 in the first innings and 52* out of a total of 85 for 7 in the second innings. On a bowler's wicket he faced the famous Aubrey Faulkner in top form, but survived, showing grit and determination as well as talent. This encounter laid the foundations for their later relationship of pupil-teacher at Faulkner's famous cricket school in London.

Although cricket was obviously his main claim to sporting fame at the college, he was also a high-class racquets player representing Cheltenham as first string in the Public Schools competition during his period there. It was felt that with hard practice he could become a champion. His name appears on many occasions during his time at the College when *The Times* dedicated generous space to public school competitions. In April 1922 when playing against Radley it was noted that "KS Duleepsinhji who played such brilliant cricket last year, is a player of both brains and brilliance." It also commented that "He made some beautiful strokes and saw the ball very quickly. It is almost impossible to believe from his figure and movement that he was still only a boy of 15; he appeared to be many years older than that, both in deportment and power." In fact Duleep was 16 at the time, so this error must have come from the incorrect date of birth on his registration form on entry to the college. In 1923 he reached the final of the Public School competition before being beaten by DS Milford of Rugby.

In the semi-final he defeated JW Greenstock of Malvern when his serving was outstanding "and he quite out-generalled his opponent". In the final at the Queen's Club *The Times* comments on his great judgment in volleying the length services. He apparently fought hard, but in view of his batting and fielding prowess it is strange to note that "he is decidedly slow on his feet" but he did have "a beautiful wrist and a good eye". Later in the year in a doubles win over Clifton "he was easily the best player of the four", using the angles in the slow Cheltenham court "very effectively". In a preview of the schools' knock-out competition when Cheltenham were drawn against the RNC, Dartmouth, he was described as a lazy player, but if he were to go out to dominate the court "he might upset all reasonable theories". The writer felt that he had some wonderful shots at his command, but must pay more attention to his footwork - is this the same person as the cricketer with the dazzling dancing feet? Later in the championships Cheltenham beat Winchester with Duleep serving three aces to win the game, but when they played Radley the correspondent noted that Duleep could not carry the game on his own against two such class performers as Dawney and Blair. "There was no weak spot to find in Duleepsinhji and so the Radley pair played cold tactics, and peppered Leigh unmercifully."

When he went on to Cambridge there is a reference to him in 1926 playing against DS Milford once more and once again losing. It was noted that he had shown great promise as a racquets player when at Cheltenham and with good coaching and plenty of practice he would obviously become a good player. Unfortunately he gave up for two years and still tended to play the ball off the wrong leg, but when meeting pace with pace could still play very brilliantly.

His final school report spoke of his character and sporting prowess: "He has really done splendidly both as captain of the XI and otherwise. He has really taken command without any fuss or display and with much consideration and courtesy. I hope often to see him here and shall greatly miss those games of racquets with him. A most honourable and useful school career."

In a publication called *Then and Now* which was an anniversary celebration of Cheltenham College 1841-1991, he gains a pride of place amongst the most celebrated of the college's alumni.

"One of the most famous of all college sportsmen came to the school. This was Kumar Shri Duleepsinhji, sent to Cheltenham possibly at the behest of Uncle Prince Ranji to benefit from Woofie's coaching. He came with cousin Ramsinhji and did not join a boarding house, but stayed with Montague Seaton in his house... His cricket at college is legendary."

It then goes on to relate a story showing how his princely upbringing in India had led him to certain assumptions about life in England. Duleepsinhji was 14 when he came to Cheltenham. On his first day at College he went into Darter's, the college bookshop, to order a book. He returned at 11.30 the next morning and was surprised to find that the book was not there. When told that the book had been ordered but had not yet arrived, he wanted to know why an assistant had not gone to London to fetch it! This was not arrogance on his part, but purely the result of his background.

In the cricket pavilion at the College there is a section devoted to his prowess with a tribute from Old Cheltonian EM Wellings, the writer and Oxford Blue, who was happy to say that with good health he would have outshone Hammond. He described him as the terror of leg-spinners and not even Bradman was quicker or more sure in his footwork. Moreover, he was second only to Hammond as a slip-fielder.

After leaving Cheltenham in summer 1923 Duleep had hoped to go to Cambridge University in the October but his uncle decided that a year out would be of benefit. As a result he did not take up his place at Clare College until October 1924. His ambition, and that of his uncle, was that he should play county cricket, but for whom? By this time Ranji's great Sussex colleague CB Fry had become his guardian, so his house in Hampshire gave him a residential qualification for that county. His uncle lived in Middlesex, so that was another possibility. However, Duleep's ambition to follow in his uncle's footsteps and play for Sussex led to Ranji organising accommodation for him in Eastbourne with his old colleague, Dr WG Heasman, and thus begin a two-year residential qualification for the county. The county and England captain, Arthur Gilligan, was delighted to welcome him.

It is of interest, however, that the minutes of the Sussex County Cricket Club, July 20, 1922 have the following entry: "A letter was received from Mr AF Somerset to say that the Maharajah of Nawanagar was very anxious for his nephew, now at Cheltenham College, to play for the county. The Secretary was instructed to make further enquiries."

This appears to be the first time that there was some official link with Duleep's name and the Sussex County Club. Perhaps mindful of this important piece of initiative, it is recorded in the Sussex minutes of February 29, 1924, that the committee elected Mr. Somerset to be a Vice-President of the county club!

Strangely there seems to be a twelve-month gap in the next stage at committee level as not until August 25, 1923 does the subject appear again. After rejecting approaches from Glamorgan and Northamptonshire to reconsider their decision not to have fixtures with them, we find that "the Secretary was instructed to write to KSD, the nephew of the Jam of Nawanagar, and ask him if he would be willing to qualify for Sussex in due course." The Committee report for 1925 reports that "in July it is hoped that strength will be imparted by the qualification of KS Duleepsinhji."

3.

CAMBRIDGE UNIVERSITY AND BEGINNING OF SUSSEX CAREER

DULEEP'S FIRST-CLASS career began in season 1924 with four games, all non-competitive, but he played in a certain amount of high standard club cricket with much success. In this his two centuries and five fifties in ten completed innings gave him 680 runs at an average of 68.00, figures which excited the county and its followers.

His debut in first-class cricket came at the end of June when he played at Lord's for the M.C.C. against Oxford University. He made two reasonable scores of 37 and 35 and also took the wicket of JL Guise in each innings. Guise, who had achieved fame with his 278 for Winchester v Eton in 1921, was to be captain of Oxford in 1925 when he dismissed Duleep in his first Cambridge v Oxford game. Immediately after this game he made his first appearance for Sussex when he failed in each innings at Hove in the game with Cambridge University; this led to certain Sussex officials wondering what all the fuss was about. The sceptics received their answer in no uncertain terms when the following day Duleep returned to Lord's to play once more for the MCC. This time his opponents were once again Cambridge

University and Duleep, opening the innings, scored his maiden first-class century. His 120 in less than three hours was described by *Wisden* as "the feature of the match". This magnificent innings included a partnership with the great Patsy Hendren of 158 in eighty-five minutes. This innings, "without a mistake of any kind", was bound to lead to memories of and comparisons with Ranji as can be seen in a report at the time. "The batting of KS Duleepsinhji was very pleasant to watch. His on-side play is brilliant: but in time he will understand that the Jam Sahib, ie Ranji, used the on-side to a great extent to draw fielders from the off-side, where he really preferred making his runs. That is by the way." In his debut match for the MCC v Oxford University it was observed that he had such a preference for the on-side that "he seemed so obsessed with the leg side that he set his feet to hit the ball there before the ball was bowled". This precluded his driving pitched-up balls on the off-side which "the Jam Sahib would have hit for four".

His 43 in the second innings of the Cambridge University match served once more to underline his outstanding class and potential. He even opened the bowling in the first innings, but was less successful. His final appearance of the season came at Hastings in September when he played for The Rest of England against Lord Cowdray's XI. He was dismissed cheaply but in his four games that season he had shown why he was considered such a prospect.

The next stage in his development would be his cricket career at Cambridge University and the

1925 season was eagerly awaited after his admission into Clare College in October 1924. Clare was a college with great tradition as it was founded in 1326 which makes it the second oldest surviving college at the university. It is famous for its chapel choir and for its gardens which back onto the River Cam. It also has a very famous bridge with fourteen stone balls decorating it, one of which has a missing section. The most commonly given reason for this is that the original builder was not paid the requisite amount for his work and so removed the segment to compensate for the missing payment!

The college has had several famous alumni over the years from all walks of life. There are such celebrated historical figures as the martyred bishop Hugh Latimer from the Tudor era, and Lord Cornwallis, British general at the time of the American Revolutionary War. Coming to more modern times we have personalities from the world of literature, as for example Peter Ackroyd and Siegfried Sassoon, the celebrated naturalist David Attenborough, musicians of the calibre of John Rutter, the composer, and Sir Roger Norrington, the conductor. Politicians and entertainers are represented by Peter Lilley and Richard Stilgoe, but the greatest cricketer is undoubtedly Duleep.

He made his first appearance in the Freshmen's match in early May. Playing for HJ Enthoven's side against that of CT Bennett, he took most of the honours in a low-scoring victory in difficult conditions with innings of 99 and 40* in the eight-wicket win. "At his first opportunity he fulfilled the high promise shown at Cheltenham and practically made himself sure of his Blue." His leg-side play was commented on as was the power and certainty of his well-timed forcing strokes. One experienced observer felt that in spite of the weight of expectation upon him he never lost his confidence, playing "some of the best cricket seen in this match for a long time". To add to his delight two of his Old Cheltonian colleagues appeared for CT Bennett's XI, MR Formby and ETLR Heywood, who was their most successful batsman.

Duleep's first game for Cambridge was, ironically, against Sussex, the county for whom he was qualifying. In the same week as the Freshmen's Trial match, the wicket was again disappointing with the University winning by 40 runs after neither side had managed to reach 100 in the first innings. In Cambridge's second innings Duleep made the second highest score of 40 after earlier catching Sussex captain Arthur Gilligan brilliantly at slip to add to his growing reputation in that area. The visit of Lancashire in a twelve-a-side game would have resulted in a victory for the Northerners had they not had to finish early to catch their train home! The burly spinner Dick Tyldesley took eleven wickets in the game, including Duleep in each innings. In the first innings he was trapped lbw for a "duck" but made what was comfortably the highest score of 55 in the second innings in a fine display of batting.

A fortnight later Yorkshire, the County Champions, came to Fenner's and, just as

Lancashire had done, played virtually their strongest side - how different from the practice in recent years when even touring Test sides are confronted with the second team whilst the first team "rests". The Yorkshire attack was made up of Emmott Robinson, Abe Waddington, Wilfred Rhodes and Roy Kilner, but Duleep's class was shown in his scores of 53 and 70, the highest in each innings. He was awarded his Blue after the first innings in only his third game. The experienced visitors were said to be highly impressed, rating him the best young amateur batsman they had seen since the end of the war; but they were not too pleased at having to concede a first-innings lead of 31 to the students in a game which finished up as a draw.

Duleep received many letters of congratulation upon receiving his Blue of which there are about twenty extant. Particularly quick off the mark was the great CB Fry, partner of Uncle Ranji in so many great stands for Sussex at the turn of the century. He wrote as follows:

HAMBLE,
HANTS.

TEL. 7 HAMBLE.
May 29.25

My dear Duleep,

I am ever so glad you have your Blue, dear lad - I knew it was a cert., bar bad luck in not getting into form early in the year.

55

I was in Paris with HH 9 (Ranji) I tell you <u>confidentially</u>; he is very very interested in you & your cricket, so don't mind if he pretends he isn't. <u>I know he is</u>. Also you have done a good job for India in proving your worth as you have.

You won't mind my giving you some advice I know you don't need.

Don't listen to flattery nor popular applause. Stay as you are: sound & humble - minded & ready ever to learn & improve. Trust your own judgment: listen to advisers but trust your own judgment. No-one makes runs for you; you do it yourself: so advisers are only useful if they advise right & then its (sic) you that do the doing.

Play your own game & remember what I told you about a bowler only being able to bowl one ball at a time - every ball is playable. Never get yourself out: let the bowler do this if he can.

You have a good chance of playing for the Gents with a fair bit of luck.

Play in the 'Varsity match as you would in a match here which you wanted to help to win. It will be the easiest bowling you meet the whole season. Don't let this occasion disturb you. Take it as an ordinary match - which it is unless you endow it with extraneous terrors.

Very ??? & good luck. I hope your leg is better. It seems so. Have <u>good spikes in your boots</u>.

Love to Ram (Duleep's cousin)
Yours CBF

Amongst other letters of congratulation were ones from a Lt. Col. Foster inviting him to play for the Hampshire Hogs, from Sol Ernest, Secretary and Treasurer of the All-India Sporting Club in Johannesburg, and from his old prep school, St.Faith's, which pointed out that he was the first person from there to receive a Blue. Of particular interest was one written on June 6 from The Sports Club, St. James's Square, by that great Kent enthusiast Gerry Weigall. After giving his congratulations he said he hoped Duleep would be a better correspondent than his famous uncle and wondered which county he was going to play for, presumably hoping to tempt him to Kent!

After playing so creditably against the Test standard bowlers of Sussex, Lancashire and Yorkshire it must have seemed a welcome relief to be confronted by the much lesser challenge of the Army attack. Duleep duly obliged with a beautiful innings of 128 scored at almost a run a minute with 14 fours.

On their first match on tour after the season had finished at Fenner's, Cambridge had an extraordinary victory at the Oval against Surrey. After Jack Hobbs had scored a century in each innings, Surrey, the eventual runners-up in the Championship, declared, leaving the University to score 426 to win on the last day. This they did for the loss of only four wickets with half an hour to spare even though they had been bowled out for only 179 in the first innings. Duleep had made a top score of 51 then, but his second innings of 98 in ninety-five minutes out of 186 in partnership with EW Dawson (128) made the victory a formality. His innings was described by *Wisden* as "very brilliant" and elsewhere it was recorded that although he appeared to have a weakness on or just outside the off-stump, his all-round strokes were deemed to be magnificent with the emphasis again on his late-cutting and on-side play. *The Times* wrote that "it was one of the finest displays of batting seen in London this season. The spectators were treated to a sparkling display of free confident batting. The hook, the leg-glance, the straight-drive and the convincing off-drive through the covers were all made with a delightful ease and certainty that justified the eulogies that have been written on his masterly batting." He was "already a great batsman in embryo" and his name was discussed as a young contender for a place in the England side for the coming Australian tour to England of 1926, his slip-fielding being noted as an additional qualification. Just as Herbert Sutcliffe had been so impressed with Duleep's batting in the Yorkshire match, so was his great partner Jack Hobbs in this game. Sutcliffe believed that with the likely development there would be in his batting, he would become an asset to the England side as he appeared to have the necessary temperament to go with his natural skills. Hobbs felt that he would develop into a champion, whilst the *Daily Mail* correspondent was impressed with his "quickness of eye and perfection of body balance". The distinguished South African cricketer-turned-coach, Aubrey Faulkner, said that this innings merely confirmed what he had thought as far back as 1921 i.e. Duleep was a cricketer of the highest class and he could not imagine his not being selected for all the Tests against the 1926 Australians.

Two games later Duleep scored his first century against a county with his 130 at Bath in the game with Somerset. He was out in an unusual way as, trying to cut George Hunt, he was caught and bowled via the chest of the wicket-keeper Mervyn Hill. Before this unlikely occurrence he had, however, added further to his reputation. "By beautiful timing and confident placing he reached his hundred in as many minutes." One writer felt that he was now on the threshold dividing the good from the great with the extra power in his off-side strokes being especially notable. In this game his match bowling figures of 5-56 remained the best of his career.

After a heavy defeat at Lord's against the MCC, Cambridge came to Eastbourne to play against HDG Leveson Gower's XI in their last game before the Lord's Varsity match and the end of their season. Duleep had a good match with scores of 63 and 72, the latter in only an hour. The majesty of his stroke-play was again commented upon with the usual rider that there was still a weakness on, or just outside, the off-stump. With an improvement in this direction he would obviously become a batsman in the very first flight.

The Varsity match began on Monday, July 6th. with an attendance of almost 16,000 people! Facing a solid Oxford total of 350, Cambridge went in to bat on the second day on a rain-affected pitch. Any fears were soon allayed as

Duleep, coming in at 40-1, "met the attack with easy confidence". PF Warner was impressed with the time that Duleep seemed to have to play the ball and joined the group of critics forecasting a great future for him. He was finally smartly stumped for 75 and returned to the pavilion to a wonderful reception.

As he had not yet qualified for Sussex, he played little cricket for the rest of the season, although he was invited to play for the Gentlemen against the Players three times before the end of the season, but did little. He also played at Blackpool for the South against the North with but moderate success. These four games brought him only 124 runs in eight innings, bringing down his Cambridge average of 49.05 to 39.11, but he did achieve the landmark of over 1,000 runs in his first season and, as we have seen, made a great impression on an ever-widening audience.

In 1926 the Australian touring team under the captaincy of HL "Horseshoe" Collins came to England to defend the Ashes. As always, there was much speculation about the candidates for the England side and Duleep's name was to the forefront of the younger possibilities. He was selected to play for the South of England against them at Bristol and also for the Rest of England v England in a Test Trial at Lord's. In addition he appeared for his university against the tourists at Fenner's in the early part of the season. Although he scored a 50 in the Lord's game, for which he received the congratulations of his college publication, *Lady Clare Magazine*, he did not do enough to force his way into what was a very strong England batting line-up. His half-century pleased that great former cricketer, GL Jessop, who saw reminiscences of the great Ranji in his play, but he also noted, as had many, a certain weakness outside the off-stump. In this match he added further to his reputation as a fielder with a "miracle" one-handed catch to dismiss Roy Kilner off a fierce stroke. "Plum" Warner was not quite sure that he was ready just yet, but felt that he would be a serious candidate for the England side on their next visit to Australia.

In the second game of the Varsity season against the very strong attack of the County Champions, Yorkshire, he had again made an excellent impression against these doughty opponents. The university emerged with great credit, earning a draw from a low-scoring game in which Duleep had scored 43 out of a total of 176 in Cambridge's only innings. Although a modest score, it was the manner of it which took the eye as in a mere forty minutes against Yorkshire's best "he treated us to some really sparkling cricket, which is most hopeful for the future, as he is not likely to meet better bowling". Incidentally, in the first match of the season against Middlesex he only batted once as the game was abandoned as a result of the General Strike. After the Yorkshire game the fixture with Sussex at Fenner's did not even start because of the turbulent political situation.

The match with the Free Foresters saw Duleep score the only century of the season for Cambridge. In a closely-fought three-wicket victory his scores of 118 and 71 were crucial factors. As in the previous season he was in good form for the match with HDG Leveson Gower's XI at Eastbourne when his 96 and 40 helped Cambridge to a 65 run victory. His 96 was scored in two and a quarter hours of faultless batting "by skilful strokes against a varied attack".

The culmination of the Varsity season was, of course, the Lord's match with Oxford which was won by Cambridge in very poor weather conditions. Their 34 run victory did not owe too much to Duleep whose contributions were a mere 6 and 36. It was again noted by PF Warner that although Duleep played some nice strokes in his 36 and that his wrist work was good, "he seems to have some weakness outside the off-stump". Even though he finished at the top of the Cambridge averages with figures of 523 runs at 34.86, it is probably true to say that a little more had been expected of him, especially as he was being looked upon as a bright hope for England's future. In his first year he had been narrowly second to HJ Enthoven in the averages with 932 runs at 49.05, but due allowance must be made for the very poor weather of 1926 with its effects on pitches and outfields.

Once the Varsity match was completed, he was free to join Sussex as his qualification period was now over. He made a wonderful immediate impact on the side, with 97 on his Championship debut at Leicester being followed by 115 in his next innings against Hampshire at Hove. This was immediately followed by 76 at Eastbourne in the Surrey game and before the end of July his 132 at Hove v Middlesex confirmed that Sussex had found an out-of-the-ordinary player. Not only was his batting of such high quality with the ability to play innings of exceptional class and charm, but also his splendid fielding was a great asset to the side. In addition to being a first-class slip-fielder it was reported in *The Cricketer Annual* that "his returns from the long-field were as fine as those of any Australian". His innings against Middlesex had brought forth great praise from that illustrious opponent "Patsy" Hendren. Not surprisingly, Arthur Gilligan, his captain, had awarded him his county cap during this period and all seemed set fair for a prolific season. However, he was unable to keep up this form with any consistency and scored only two more half-centuries during the season; one for his county in the return Leicestershire game at Hastings when in his 73* his beautiful strokes, particularly his late and square cutting, were commented upon favourably, and the other in September at Scarborough for the Gentlemen against the Players. As with Cambridge he did, however, finish on the top of the averages for his county with 696 runs at 34.80 which gave a seasonal total of 1,421 runs at an average of 34.65 and a career one of 36.40. These figures, whilst reasonable, are not sufficient as yet to place him in the category of "great", but in the rest of the career he was allowed before ill-health cruelly curtailed it, we will see how the runs flowed and his reputation came to vie with that of Walter Hammond as the greatest of the rising stars of English batting. Already, however, the comparisons with Ranji were growing, even if at times slightly qualified, and there was continual reference to the masterful ease of his batting, its grace and style.

The season of 1927 was, to put it mildly, a most eventful one for Duleep, one which saw the first serious onset of the illness which was to finish his cricket career. He started off the season in tremendous form after having undergone a winter's coaching at the school of Aubrey Faulkner. Faulkner had worked very hard to improve Duleep's off-side shots and this soon began to bear fruit as in the first game of the season at Fenner's against mighty Yorkshire, who again played their best side - autres temps, autres moeurs - he scored 101 in a little over two hours when he showed a marked improvement in his off-side play "batting with delightful freedom and variety". It was said that the only fault that stood between him and greatness the previous season had been his weakness in dealing with the short ball outside the off-stump and his extra sessions with Faulkner were now showing the benefit. With not a little irony *The Times* commented that "there seems every reason for believing that this will be a good season for him". The Cambridge side came out of the match with great credit, securing an honourable draw and Duleep's second innings "duck" was soon forgotten in the next game at Fenner's against Middlesex.

After scoring 43 in the first innings he scored 254* out of 362 in the second innings in which he batted for a mere four hours, thereby beating the previous ground record of a Cambridge cricketer at Fenner's, Hubert Ashton's 236* in 1920. He hit thirty-four 4s in a display "as remarkable as it was versatile" and was noted for his ability to score runs with equal ease in <u>all directions</u>, i.e. off as well as leg. The Press was full of praise for his innings. Whilst his innings was not faultless, "it was nevertheless full of magnificent cricket" with his runs scored at an exhilarating pace. "Strong, as always, on the on-side, he made most of his runs between fine-leg and mid-on, but his cutting was beautiful to watch and in his driving the ball was hit hard and cleanly. It was altogether <u>the innings of a man who, in a few years, may be the greatest batsman in England</u>." (Author's underlining). His score remains a record for Cambridge University and for several years was the ground record for Fenner's. Pelham Warner wrote to him: "My dear Duleep, My heartiest congratulations on your splendid batting. You are indeed a credit to the Faulkner school." It is worth noting perhaps that as a conscientious scholar he attended a session with his tutor at 9 p.m. on the day he played this great innings!

However, there was only one more game for him before being overtaken by illness. The bitterly cold weather continued during the Sussex game when he scored 36 in a drawn match with Cambridge, scoring exactly double the county's score in the first innings. He had not been well after his epic innings in the Middlesex game and just after playing against Sussex he caught a chill which developed into a very serious attack of pleurisy with ominous signs of pulmonary tuberculosis. It was soon evident that he would play no more cricket that season; indeed, there was a great threat to his life and it was decided that a winter in the clean and healthy air of Switzerland would be necessary. He was sent to a sanatorium with Uncle Ranji paying his expenses. *The Cricketer* expressed its sympathy for him forecasting that with a return to health he would justify all those who had predicted a great career for him. He received many letters of encouragement from such people as Aubrey Faulkner, Pelham Warner and his club secretary, Mr WL Knowles. Aubrey Faulkner wrote to him linking him with Walter Hammond as the two young batsmen of the year. He urged him to hurry up and get well as "after all one year's cricket in twenty being missed doesn't sound too much". He thought it a "dreadful waste of time" that he had to spend a winter in Switzerland as he wanted him to attend his Christmas nets "to fix your off-side shots for good and all before next season commences. If you let me get at you during the Christmas and Easter holidays, there should be no holding you next year... you have a wonderful cricket future in front of you." Uncle Ranji sent him a Christmas card hoping for his recovery in the following season, adding " You are a great baby and want a perpetual nurse to look after you." Reports were coming from Switzerland that he was not recovering quite so quickly as had been anticipated but, nevertheless, he returned to England in the late Spring of 1928, albeit very weak and unfit to play until the warmer weather of the end of May. In the five innings that he had been able to play in 1927 he had scored 434 runs at an impressive average if 108.50.

Duleepsinhji - Prince of Cricketers

The *Lady Clare Magazine* of Easter 1927 contained a lengthy article about him under the title of "Smith", his soubriquet. It begins by referring to his time at Cheltenham College after confessing to knowing little about his early life, "but we may infer one or two facts in the light of his subsequent history. It is evident, for instance, that his nurse was a fast bowler, because he had been at Cheltenham some time before he began to score by any other strokes than late-cuts and leg-glides". He bowled leg-breaks "which used to rise to an enormous height and broke a long way when they reached earth". In his time as captain of the Day Boys they twice won the House Cup; the first time he won it almost single-handedly, bowling unchanged throughout all three matches at an average of eight runs per wicket, whilst with the bat he scored a century in all three matches averaging "between seventy and eighty". In one match he made 70 out of an all-out score of 100 and then proceeded in the second innings to make 170 out of a total of "about 230 to win". His wonderful fielding ability is also commented upon as he "used to terrify the humbler batsmen on the opposing side by fielding at silly-point and picking the ball off their bats".

After recording his further achievements as a cricketer, including his being named as the best public school bat of the year in his final year, the article comments on his fading out of the limelight in 1924 - the year he took off after leaving Cheltenham - with the rumour circulating that he was studying too hard to play cricket. "Whether this is true or not it is hard to

67

say, but the result of it all was that he passed the Little-go with flying colours and came up to Cambridge the next year."

The article goes on to mention his university cricket career to date before making a surprising double error as it writes about his "remarkable innings of 245 against Nottinghamshire". How did 254* against Middlesex come to be so confused! Great regret is expressed at his being stricken with pleurisy after this magnificent achievement, but it was felt that he was progressing satisfactorily even though he would not be able to play any more for the rest of the season.

That so much should be written about him in the college magazine is a clear indication of his standing there and the pride they took in him.

There had been a certain amount of pessimism regarding his fitness for the 1928 season with *The Cricketer* having already remarked that "it would be a thousand pities if he were to run any risk by playing too soon" and suggesting that he must wait until late May at the earliest. Cambridge would be wise not to rely upon his appearing, but if he could play, so much the better. *The Times* also was rather guarded in its issue of April 19th as it stated that "it is not expected that he will undertake any serious match play during the early part of the season, but it is hoped that he will be able to test his form in some minor games during the first weeks of the term". He made his first appearance on May 26 in the match against the touring West Indians at Fenner's. His 41 showed that he had lost none of his style with his timing and elegance being again evident.

What was clear, however, for several matches was that his long injury lay-off had sapped his strength and stamina. He seemed unable to build an innings after several promising starts, his 107 runs in the next seven innings prompting him to ask the Cambridge captain to drop him. However, Jim Seabrook was of the opinion that "form is temporary, class is permanent" and refused to consider the idea. With the Varsity game approaching Duleep started to come back to form with innings of 54 v Sussex at Hove, 96 v Leveson Gower's XI at Eastbourne and 41* v the MCC at Lord's. In his innings at Eastbourne it was reported that in the university's bid to avoid defeat "the chief interest was centred on Duleepsinhji who was batting in perfect style" but seemingly lacking support at the other end. "He made a number of splendid drives" and was looking well set for a century but with his first poor stroke he was caught in the slips four runs short. His lack of fitness was apparent in the MCC game at Lord's. As for the previous match, it was reported that the greatest interest would be taken in the batting of KS Duleepsinhji. The correspondent then went on to say that "his fielding at slip this year has been remarkable and his eye is obviously as quick and accurate as ever. He has not yet, however, got his strength back. KS Duleepsinhji sees the ball quickly enough to make the most magnificent strokes, but because the body will not immediately obey the eye and the brain he gets out playing the very strokes which the player in a lower class cannot attempt." The writer was of the opinion that in the slips he saw the ball more quickly than anyone in England, but "his limbs, however, do not quite obey his very quick eye when he is batting".

He was now coming back to his best and with increasing fitness it was apparent that his strokes were becoming far more powerful with his improvement in off-side play even more discernible. The university match finished in an exciting draw with the Dark Blues just holding on with nine wickets down. Duleep batted with "ease and confidence" for his 52 and 37 with strokes all round the wicket marked by perfect timing and wrist work. Although at times criticised for standing too close, there was again much praise for his slip-fielding, especially off the leg-break bowling of future England captain, RWV Robins. "With his agility and quickness of eye, probably no one sees the ball so soon, or so quickly, as the popular Cantab who is familiarly known in the Cambridge XI as Smith." He finished his university cricket career with 444 runs for the season at an average of 29.60, figures which gave no indication of his performances for the rest of the season.

There seems to be little known of his life off the cricket pitch or in the lecture rooms at Cambridge, but he was President of the Cambridge University Crocodiles' Club and a member of the university Burma Society. What exactly went on at these clubs seems very esoteric, but they both met at the Dorothy Café which for some time had as an exotic sweet on its menu, a certain Dessert Duleep. On June 6, 1925, it is on record that The Jam Sahib of

Nawanagar, i.e. Ranji, gave a toast to the Crocodiles' Club at its annual dinner, whilst on March 1st the following year his nephew gave one to the Burma Society.

There is a section on him in a publication called *Clare - Through The Twentieth Century* when he is named as undoubtedly "Clare's cricketer of the twentieth century". PF Warner is quoted as rating him "the most promising young batsman in England "before going on to say that he was "quite definitely a better player at his age than Ranji". After listing some of his famous exploits, referring to his illness and regretting that he did not play for England more often, his membership of the "Trundlers" is recalled. This esoteric group came into existence before World War I, seemingly organised for those undergraduates whose main pre-occupations were cricket or tennis. There was no mention of academic work in the college magazine of 1910, "despite the college being full". The most distinguishing feature of an ex-Trundler was not his cricketing ability, but the "grotesque colouring of his cap and tie, which consists of broad stripes of yellow, pink and purple." These strange colours were some sort of amalgamation with Corpus Christi and King's in the difficult times just after World War I. They played in the long summer vacations and were operating until the late 1960s, but alas with no one even vaguely approaching Duleepsinhji's class in sight.

In retrospect it seems odd that such an outstanding player and personality, who later made a great reputation as a captain in his two years in the office at Sussex, should not have captained his university. The sad truth is that in this period there was much colour prejudice at Oxford and Cambridge. Although a coloured player would not be stopped representing his university, it was considered a step too far to have him as captain, even an Indian prince! He was not elected a member of the elitist Hawks' Club in his first year, normally an automatic procedure for a "Blue". He was eventually made a member when the Cambridge captain threatened to resign and his uncle insisted. His equanimity on this occasion was astonishing as he calmly told a Clare colleague: "I do not take offence. These things will pass just as the day follows the night. There will always be human beings on this earth who think they are superior to others." This prejudice led to Asians forming the Crocodiles' Club which was restricted to Asians and those having gained school or college colours. He was very proud of his presidency, often wearing its blazer in preference to his light blue one.

On hearing of his death, Sir Henry Thirkill, one of his contemporaries at Clare, spoke for all who had known him as a student. He highlighted his charm and courtesy, his ease of manner, natural modesty and humility, integrity and strength of character, all attributes as he said which later in life made him such an ideal representative for India as High Commissioner to Australia. He went on to say that even after so many years back in India, his letters showed his life-long interest in cricket and his great affection for Clare College.

When he rejoined Sussex in mid-July, his form was phenomenal as, with strength restored, he proceeded to produce consistently those scores which his legions of admirers had always foreseen. As *Wisden* stated, "Driving harder than hitherto, and more sure in his forcing strokes to the off, Duleepsinhji developed quite to the extent anticipated, and, with increased physical strength, he must become a great power in the eleven." His Sussex season began with an innings of 121 at Eastbourne against Glamorgan when he reached his century before lunch. This was followed by 198 at Kettering in the Northamptonshire match scored at a run a minute, thus helping to give his bowlers plenty of time to accomplish an innings victory. Once again "his splendidly-timed driving" was emphasised in the match report. His 125 at Hove against Middlesex, when he "scored brilliantly all round the wicket", participating in a stand of 214 with Bowley in less than three hours, was a leading feature of a high-scoring draw. Before the end of August he had scored further centuries with 107 against Kent, 150 against a Somerset side containing nine amateurs and, most impressive of all, 150 in the Yorkshire match at Eastbourne. Set against this were failures in the matches with Nottinghamshire and Lancashire when the speed of Larwood and McDonald proved too much. September proved to be a satisfactory month with three half-centuries in five innings including two at Scarborough against the MCC side due to go to Australia that winter.

His surge at the end of the season had come just too late to give him a realistic chance of being included in the MCC side which was announced as early as the end of July; moreover, there may have been still some doubts about his fitness to undertake such a long and strenuous tour.

In his eleven matches for his county he had scored 1,082 runs at an average of 60.11 with six centuries, the most by a Sussex player that season in fewer than half the games played by any of the other batsmen. Arthur Gilligan, his captain, pleased with the progress shown by his side, singled out Duleep for particular praise affirming that Sussex had at last found a great number three batsman. His overall record for the season was 1,706 runs at an average of 47.38, whilst his career average was steadily rising with an average of 42.34 for 4,870 runs. Even better was to come!

4.

K.S. DULEEPSINHJI, CAMBRIDGE UNIVERSITY, SUSSEX and ENGLAND

IN THE WINTER OF 1928 Duleep returned to his homeland for the first time since he had started his education in England. He had gone to see his family, but was soon subjected to approaches from the newly-formed Indian Cricket Board of Control to become more involved in Indian cricket as there had been tentative arrangements for a tour to England in 1932 when they would play their first-ever Test. In fact, when he was in New Zealand with the MCC side the following winter he received an official approach from the President of the Board to be their captain if invited. Although he was by that time an England player, he was assured by the President that the Board had been given to understand "that there will be no difficulty in obtaining the necessary permission from England for you to play for India".

He played in one match at the Bombay Gymkhana ground for the Hindus against the Parsees in the Quadrangular tournament. His scores of 84 and 38 showed a large and enthusiastic crowd why he had gained such a reputation in England with elegant strokes at a rapid run-rate. To try to restrict his rapid scoring, spin-bowler Jamshedji proceeded to bowl wide outside the off-stump to a packed off-side field. After carefully weighing up the situation Duleep proceeded to use what we now term the reverse sweep, much to the bowler's consternation. He appealed to the umpire, Joe Birtwhistle, to give Duleep out for using unfair means! The umpire pointed out that he had broken no rules, he had just cleverly improvised.

He did not return to England for the 1929 season until the middle of May, thus missing Sussex's first three matches and the early season cold weather. Thanks to Ranji's generosity, however, Duleep was allowed to carry on playing. In his third game against Lancashire at Old Trafford he scored a scintillating 134 in just under two hours. His innings was described as "dazzling" and "worth walking many miles to see". Sussex's 466 on the opening day was in stark contrast to the previous match at the ground when "The Battle of the Roses" had produced its usual war of attrition. Sussex with their enterprise had deservedly gained a wonderful victory against the reigning champions by an innings and 95 runs with Duleep adding three slip-catches to his century. After scoring 82 and 28 at Derby, Duleep was invited to play at Lord's for MCC against the touring South Africans. He did his England chances no harm with 74 and 27* in a drawn game. His first innings was a typical one when he scored his runs out of 119 in an hour, showing his full range of strokes. The signs that he was in the mind of the Test selectors came the following week when he was chosen for the

Test Trial at Lord's as a member of the Rest side v England. Although his scores were a modest 41 and 2, he had done enough to convince the selectors that he deserved his chance in the England XI and he was chosen to play against South Africa at Edgbaston in the first Test. His invitation to play in this Test came from a very informal hand-written letter addressed "My dear Duleep" and signed "Shrimp" i.e. Chairman of Selectors, HDG Leveson Gower.

Also making his debut for England in this Test was the 22-year-old Cambridge University player ET Killick, who won his "Blue" in the seasons 1928 to 1930. He played for Middlesex from 1926-39 but his appearances were strictly limited as he became a clergyman. He played in only 92 first-class games, but with 5,730 runs at an average of 40.35 and 15 centuries, including three double, it is clear that he could have become a player of the highest class, perhaps the David Sheppard of his time. As a matter of interest, the rest of the England side was H SUTCLIFFE, WR HAMMOND, EH HENDREN, M LEYLAND, PGH FENDER, MW TATE, H LARWOOD, JC WHITE (capt.) and G DUCKWORTH - a very strong combination.

Making his debut for South Africa was Bruce Mitchell who was to become one of their greatest players. In this match he showed from the beginning that stubbornness and resolution for which he was to become so famous as his innings of 88 and 61* lasted in total nine and a half hours!

The match eventually fizzled out into a draw, the highlights being second innings centuries by Sutcliffe and Hammond, five wickets in South

Africa's first innings by Larwood, and for the visitors first-wicket century stands in each innings by Bob Catterall and Mitchell.

Unfortunately, Duleep failed in each innings with scores of 12 and 1. Although he could reasonably have expected to be given another chance in the next Test at Lord's, he was not, in fact, chosen for any other Test that summer, nor even for the Gentlemen v the Players, even though along with RES Wyatt he was the outstanding amateur batsman of the season. Would success in this fixture have caused embarrassment to the selectors? What makes these omissions so surprising is that his form after this Test was exceptional as in one period of about six weeks he scored six centuries, two of them double, at almost a run a minute with superb stroke-play. There is a "conspiracy" theory which Duleep subscribed to that people high in the game were uneasy with an Indian playing for England - even though his uncle had with such great distinction - and were also mindful of political considerations with South Africa being the opponents. It appears that, as with Ranji, the ubiquitous Lord Harris was behind the move to keep him out as another "bird of passage". There was no doubt that he was eligible to play for England as is shown by a study of the rules laid down by the Imperial Cricket Conference in 1909. These stated that a cricketer may elect to play for any country in which he is residing and has resided for not less than four years immediately preceding and that thereafter he shall always be eligible to play for that country. Duleep, therefore, was perfectly entitled to play for England. It was rumoured that the South African team were not happy with his inclusion in the side, but this was strenuously denied by their captain, HG Deane, who wrote to Duleep telling him that none of the South African party, management or players, had any objection to his presence in the England team.

His continued omission from the England side and his non-selection for the Gentlemen caused great controversy throughout the country as he was a most popular player and personality. Aubrey Faulkner wrote to him to express his disgust at the scandalous way in which he had been treated. "Your omission from the Tests is a blemish on English cricket. The affair is damnably unjust to you." Duleep himself was so upset that he seriously contemplated retiring from the game.

In the somewhat controversial match between Sussex and Essex at Leyton the feature of the game was an innings of 202 by Duleep in less than three hours. PF Warner commented on the fact that although he scored at such a great rate, there was nothing frenzied about his batting, it was just a matter of playing each ball on its perceived merits with little or no apparent risk. The controversy arose through the failure of Arthur Gilligan, the Sussex captain, to declare on the last day when his side finished with a lead of over 500. This was the first of three centuries in four games as against Derbyshire at Hove he scored 118 in Sussex's innings victory when he added 197 in two hours with Harold Gilligan, whose 143 was his maiden century, with Duleep "rather overshadowing his partner", and against

Hampshire at Bournemouth his second innings score of 112 out of an all-out total of 220 was described by *Wisden* as "a wonderfully fine display". In the game between the Essex and Derbyshire fixtures Sussex played Kent at Maidstone on a wicket which had been deliberately watered after a very hot spell. The great Kent spinner, "Tich" Freeman, was in his element with 7-16 and 6-89 and the game ended before lunch on the second day. Duleep was furious and promised Lord Harris, that great and influential figure at Kent and the MCC, that he would score a century in each innings in the return fixture at Hastings.

This kind of boasting was most untypical of the modest young Indian, but he was true to his word and, in fact, did even better with scores of 115 and 246 in his county's 167 run victory, his six catches serving to underline his efforts with the bat. He became only the fifth batsman to achieve this particular feat and only failed by three runs to score 100 on three consecutive days. His glorious batting in each innings, with his runs gathered at such a breath-taking pace, drew superlatives from the press and friend and foe alike. The correspondent for *The Times* declared that his innings was one of the finest seen at the Hastings ground "or any other ground, and definitely places him among the great batsmen of all time". Are the italicised words hyperbole, or do they represent the legitimate, considered opinion of a reporter writing for a much-respected newspaper? He had a spell in the second innings when he went "berserk" with fours and the occasional six coming "almost too quick to tally". Although "superlatives are dangerous...they can be applied to KS Duleepsinhji's innings", the reporter went on. His 246 contained five 6s and thirty-one 4s making "thousands of people happy in the process". He had reached his second century with a "glorious six" off Woolley and he continued to gather runs in the late sunshine "like a bee gathers honey". Nobody had seen Freeman that season played with such contemptuous ease, a season in which the Kent spinner eventually took 267 wickets at 18.27 each. In the previous season he had taken 304 wickets, which remains the record, and in the following three seasons after 1929 he had 275, 276 and 253 victims. Many wondered just why Duleep had been left out of the Test side. Freeman himself said at the end of the innings that he had never seen in all his career such a wonderful display of batsmanship; "It didn't matter whether I bowled a good length or pitched them short, he gave me the finest leather hunt I shall ever have." He then went straight into the Sussex dressing-room to congratulate Duleep warmly.

Sussex's next home game was against Lancashire towards the end of August in what was the first of two games in the first-ever County Festival at Eastbourne. At the Saffrons, to the background noise of croquet being played, Duleep, "slim, quick-moving, with a hint of wizardry and magic about him", once again played an innings of great charm with a score of 122. Sussex were only thwarted by the efforts of Harry Makepeace who, on a turning wicket on the last day, showed that obduracy for which he was famous and held out for over two hours whilst all around him were falling. Duleep's batting against the formidable Lancashire spinner, Dick Tyldesley, had been a masterful effort. In the second game of the festival in a drawn match with Nottinghamshire he scored a fluent 64 in his county's only innings before falling victim to Harold Larwood.

He was chosen for three matches in the end of season Scarborough Festival with mixed fortunes. He had a double failure for CI Thornton's XI v the South Africans and 36 and 55 run out for Lord Hawke's XI v the MCC Australian team. He finished off the season, however, with another magnificent performance. Playing for the MCC v Yorkshire his second innings score of 167* was described in *Wisden* as a "superb display, marked early on by much care and later on by extreme brilliancy". This was a most exciting game won by Yorkshire whose 102 for 6 was scored with only two minutes to spare off 16.3 overs. Ironically, Duleep's brilliance had given Yorkshire the chance to win as his superb batting gave MCC enough runs to set up a declaration! He batted "with exquisite artistry and the justest sense of proportion". Some of his shots could have looked dangerous if attempted by normal players, but "for him they were as safe as they used to be for his illustrious uncle. For the rest one does not know which is the more admirable, his discretion in choosing his shots or his mastery in the execution of them." He had decided that he would try and make a declaration possible and "grasped the opportunity greedily. The variety of his strokes was as near as may be infinite. For instance, a short, fast ball that rose head high was smashed as they smash a lob at lawn tennis."

The Cricketer summed up his season as follows: "When KS Duleepsinhji was at the wicket, the game was magnetised almost as in the era of his uncle, KS Ranjitsinhji, for the brilliance of his batting was not only magnificent, but the rest of the eleven learnt much by watching his methods." His two innings at Hastings with his mastery of Freeman were emphasised as was his brilliance in the slips. All his centuries up to this point had been scored in under two hours. He finished the season with 2,545 runs at 53.02 and eight centuries.

His performances in the season led to his being chosen as one of *Wisden's* Five Cricketers of the Year in the 1930 edition along with fellow amateurs RES Wyatt and RWV Robins, South African HG Owen-Smith and county colleague EH Bowley. He was described in the article as being a wonderfully well-equipped run-getter with great footwork and, like Ranji, he had a remarkable eye and supple wrists. His perceived weakness in off-side play had been overcome and he could clearly be regarded as being accomplished enough to be one of the great batsmen of the younger generation. His splendid slip-fielding was acknowledged as was the general surprise at his failure to be selected for the Gentlemen against the Players at Lord's.

5.

AUSTRALIA and
NEW ZEALAND 1929/30

FOR THE FIRST TIME since 1891/92 two England sides went out in the winter of 1929/30 to contest Test series. In 1891 Lord Sheffield's side under the captaincy of WG Grace had gone to Australia, losing the Test series 2-1, whilst a team led by WW Read of Surrey went to South Africa, winning the only Test by the decisive margin of an innings and 189 runs. In 1929/30, with England touring sides by now under the auspices of the MCC since 1903/04, one side went to the West Indies under the leadership of the Hon. FSG Calthorpe, whilst the other went to Australia and New Zealand. The original choice of captain for this team had been Duleep's captain at Sussex, AER Gilligan, but when he decided he was unfit, the captaincy went to his brother AHH Gilligan, also of Sussex. Duleep was selected for this tour and was joined by county colleagues Ted Bowley and "Tich" Cornford to make it a foursome from Hove. W. Findlay, Secretary of the MCC, stipulated in his official invitation that he had to make an appointment with a Dr. Donald Mackinnon at 78 Hamilton Terrace, NW8 during July for a medical examination. Transport, laundry and tips would be paid for, but not "smokes and drinks". The letter was addressed to the home of Dr WG Heasman of Michael Grove, Eastbourne, which was, of course, the residence found for him by Ranji to enable him to play for Sussex.

Although England could turn out two high-quality touring sides, it was notable that many leading cricketers, such as WR Hammond, H Sutcliffe, JB Hobbs, MW Tate and H Larwood did not go on either trip. The New Zealand authorities had been insistent that Duleep should be in the party to visit their country, so much had they heard of his attractive batsmanship and they were certainly not disappointed. In fact they had insisted that Duleep and either Frank Woolley or Patsy Hendren should be part of the side, an invitation accepted by Woolley, whilst Hendren went to the West Indies where he had a remarkably successful season. He scored 1,765 runs at an incredible average of 135.76 with six centuries in eighteen innings, including four doubles. So popular was he with the West Indian crowds that it is said that many children born around that period were named Patsy in his honour!

The first part of the tour consisted of games against all five of the major cricketing states. The honours were shared with wins against Western Australia and South Australia, losses against Victoria and Queensland and a draw with New South Wales. The features of this last game were high scores from Australia's up-and-coming champions, Don Bradman and Archie Jackson, and an even higher one (219) from England's great veteran, Frank Woolley. So impressive was

Jackson that some of the MCC side thought that he would make more runs in England than Bradman. Duleep's contributions were consistent, but lacking the large scores which were coming to be expected. His 64* in the South Australia match was described as an innings which "showed his most brilliant form". He also scored fifties in two of the other games and just failed in a third finishing with an average of almost 40 for this part of the tour. He was, however, disappointed with himself for repeatedly being dismissed when seemingly well set.

Although he had not scored as heavily as he had hoped in Australia, he had still left an indelible impression on those who had seen him. The celebrated Australian cricket writer, AG Moyes, called him a "batsman of undiluted charm, lithe, almost delicate looking, but speedy of foot with that quicker eye-sight which is the heritage of his race, a glorious stroke-player... a batsman of quality."

MCC then crossed the Tasman Sea to New Zealand to play their first game there at Wellington. Duleep's 96 in the second innings was "a very free display" with his cutting singled out for particular praise. After three failures he then took part in New Zealand's first-ever Test at Christchurch. England's win by eight wickets was notable for the achievement of Maurice Allom who in his eighth over of his first Test took four wickets in five balls, including a hat-trick. Duleep's contribution was a very sound one of 49 - the highest score of the game - and 33*, together with three sharp slip-catches.

The second Test at Wellington was drawn with Duleep batting well for 40 and 56*, the highest aggregate of any England player. The honours of the game, however, fell to Frank Woolley and the New Zealand opening pair of JE Mills and CS Dempster. The Kent all-rounder took 7-76 in the first innings and two of the four wickets to fall in the second innings. For New Zealand Mills and Dempster opening the innings put on 276 recording the first centuries in Test cricket by New Zealand batsmen. Duleep once again took three catches, all off Woolley.

In between the second and third Tests Duleep played a memorable innings in a minor game at Napier against Hawkes Bay when he scored 242 in just over four hours with 42 fours. After the drawn game with Auckland when he was run out for 69 came the rain-ruined Test at that ground. The first two days were completely washed out leaving only day three. This was sufficient, however, for Duleep to play a most memorable innings. His maiden Test century of 117 was described as "dazzling cricket, surpassing anything seen in recent years in New Zealand". Footwork, timing and placement were all commented upon, but perhaps best of all was the comparison with Victor Trumper when he had exhibited his genius in that country. England declared on 330 for 4, fellow Sussex player Ted Bowley also scoring a century, leaving New Zealand to score 96 for 1 in the time remaining. What is remarkable when comparing this with modern Tests is that during the day no fewer than 122 overs were bowled, over a third more than is expected today from our finely-tuned athletes.

An extra Test was arranged at Auckland to try to make up for the disappointment of the weather-stricken game. This was a high-scoring draw with Duleep scoring a relatively restrained 63. The England hero on this occasion was Geoffrey Legge with his 196, which I believe was the highest score for England by a Kent player until beaten by Robert Key in 2004.

Duleep finished the tour with his reputation, if anything, enhanced. It was not only the runs but the way in which he made them that so delighted the New Zealand crowds. His personal charm also had a great effect on his popularity. Two of his fellow tourists summed up his character thus: "Kumar Shri Duleepsinhji; Honourable Prince, Mr Very Generous Lion Esquire." His reputation on and off the field and the impression he made are clearly seen in a letter written several years later in October 1936. In a letter to the Maharajah of Nawanagar, Duleep's brother, Mr AE Donnelly, Chairman of the New Zealand Cricket Council, and writing on its behalf, said that Duleep was the "best-liked cricketer who has come to New Zealand... I have always regarded him as being the best sportsman who has played Test cricket in either England or Australia since the War."

He was the leading run-scorer on the tour with an average of 59.20 in all matches and a Test average of 89.50.

6.

1930 SUSSEX RECORD
AND TRIUMPHS AT LORD'S

AFTER A RESPECTABLE 35 at Trent Bridge in his first game of the season Duleep broke the record individual score for Sussex which had been set by his uncle Ranji in 1901. His 285* v Somerset at Taunton was eclipsed by Duleep's innings of 333 at Hove off the Northamptonshire attack scored in only five-and-a-half hours, "his stroke-play all round the wicket being magnificent". Duleep gave "a brilliant display of batting" and, timing the ball with utter certainty, drove with power on either side of the wicket. His time at the crease was also notable for glorious square cutting. "Continuing to do as he pleased with the bowling, KS Duleepsinhji, amidst great enthusiasm, beat the record individual score made for Sussex." He was eventually stumped after a faultless innings when advancing down the pitch. The Sussex total was notable also for a partnership between Duleep and Maurice Tate of 255 in a mere 105 minutes with no other player scoring as many as 20. His innings was recorded on a fine new scoreboard, donated to the county by the sons of a great Sussex enthusiast, Sir Hildebrand Hamsworth, and being used for the very first time. The legendary umpire Frank Chester gave his opinion several years later that he had never seen anything to compare with this innings, not even from Bradman. Records are made to be broken and 73 years later on the same ground Murray Goodwin scored 335* against Leicestershire.

In mid-May the Australian touring team made their first appearance of the season at Lord's in the MCC match. After his fine performances during the previous season and in Australasia during the winter there was much interest in Duleep's inclusion for the game. He did not disappoint his supporters as his only innings of 92, ended by a brilliant stumping, was comfortably the highest individual score of the match. It was reported that Duleep's effort should encourage England as he showed that "there is nothing phenomenal nor even anything exceptional about the Australian bowling". His play was marked by cuts and leg-side strokes, with the occasional off-side boundary from seeming defensive strokes, such was his timing. To help his cause even more, his slip-catch to dismiss the visitors' vice-captain, VY Richardson, was exceptional.

On returning to Fenner's later in the month for Sussex his 147 in under three hours against the University was another example of brilliant strokes all round the wicket. In what was the traditional Whitsuntide Bank Holiday fixture with Middlesex at Lord's, Duleep repeated his 1929 feat of a century in each innings of a county match with scores of 116 and 102*. Playing "very sound and flawless cricket", he was matched by his 1926 Cambridge captain, HJ Enthoven, whom he caught in each innings, who scored 123 and 115 for Middlesex in a drawn game.

Although there had been opposition from Lord Harris who seemed to have far too much influence on English cricket, Duleep was selected in the England XIII for the first Test at Trent Bridge. As a reminder, Duleep was fully qualified to play for England, and had indeed already done so several times, under rules passed at the Imperial Cricket Conference at Lord's in 1909; moreover, the Australians had not raised any objections. In passing one may add that GOB Allen, who played one Test for England in the series, was born in Sydney, Australia, AA Jackson who played in two Tests for Australia was born in Scotland and CV Grimmett, playing in all five Tests for Australia, was born in New Zealand. Previously C Bannerman, PS McDonnell, H Carter and W Midwinter had all played for Australia, although they were born in England.

In the event, Duleep was left out of the side and made twelfth man, a part that he played with distinction when he fielded all day on the last day, substituting for the injured Sutcliffe. His omission caused the outspoken critic EHD Sewell to denounce the selectors for leaving out a man of Duleep's class with the bat and in the field, in a team which was already so short of all-round fielding ability.

The next two games for Sussex saw Duleep achieve moderate success, but then came the highlight of his career. He was again included in the XIII for the second Test at Lord's and, after Sutcliffe's withdrawal through injury, was included in the final side. This Test, which Australia eventually won by seven wickets, must go down as one of the greatest ever, a game in which Duleep played a major part. England won the toss and batted, losing Jack Hobbs and Frank Woolley after a brilliant cameo of an innings, with the total on 53. To tremendous applause this brought in Duleep to join Walter Hammond and how well he repaid the wonderful faith which the ordinary cricket follower had in him! Following in the footsteps of his legendary uncle, he made a century in his first Test against Australia and in so doing made what was at the time the highest score by an England player in a Lord's Test. His 173 was a masterly display, characterised by late and square cutting and on-driving. A fascinating feature of the innings was his duel with that great Australian spinner Clarrie Grimmett, whose wiles were countered by Duleep's lightning footwork. He played Grimmett so well that he had to be taken off. The press was unanimous in its praise, which could not have been given to a more popular cricketer. Uncle Ranji was moved to say that through his nephew's innings he had relived his own cricketing days: "I am the proudest man in England," he said to a colleague out of Duleep's hearing, "I have realised one of my greatest ambitions and am basking in reflected glory."

It was not a chanceless innings, however, as he was badly missed by Australian captain Bill Woodfull on 65 and from a sharper chance by Tim Wall. In the midst of all this praise there was a certain degree of criticism concerning the manner of his dismissal. Towards the end of the day he was attacking the bowling with an element of recklessness which led to his being caught on the boundary by Bradman a quarter of an hour from the close. With the benefit of hindsight it can be said that if he had played to the end of the day, England would not have lost. As one can imagine, Bradman himself, whilst full of praise for his innings, did think that he had "thrown it away". Ranji himself, watching the innings from his private box, was naturally thrilled, but is alleged to have said that "the boy was always careless". In the second innings he made an impressive 48, with several examples of his graceful driving before being brilliantly caught down the leg-side by Oldfield off the bowling of the left-arm Hornibrook. The press was in no doubt about Duleep's achievement with headlines such as "Magic of Duleep at Lord's" and "A Wizard from the East". That great Australian batsman of the previous era, Charlie Macartney, described it as an innings that " one will cherish".

Having highlighted Duleep's part in the match, it would perhaps be appropriate to try to justify its reputation as one of the most memorable Tests ever. The fact it was played at Lord's, then more than now perhaps, the very centre of world cricket, gives it an extra distinction, and one cannot but be impressed (perhaps even over-awed!) by the extraordinary talent on view. The England batting order of JB HOBBS, FE WOOLLEY, WR HAMMOND, KS DULEEPSINHJI, EH HENDREN, APF CHAPMAN, GOB ALLEN, MW TATE, RWV ROBINS, JC WHITE and G DUCKWORTH was opposed by the equally impressive Australian one of WM WOODFULL, WH PONSFORD, DG BRADMAN, AF KIPPAX, SJ McCABE, VY RICHARDSON, WA OLDFIELD, AG FAIRFAX, CV GRIMMETT, PM HORNIBROOK and TW WALL. At a conservative estimate at least half those on view would be candidates for their country's best-ever eleven, with those such as Hobbs, Hammond and Bradman automatic choices. The weather was superb throughout and the total attendance for the match of over 110,000 ensured that there would be a large, appreciative audience. For the first time in England all the Tests in the series were given four-day status, which was just as well as this game did not finish until shortly after five o'clock on the last day.

On the opening day England scored just over 400 for the loss of nine wickets, the next best score to Duleep's 173 being 54 by his Sussex teammate, Maurice Tate. When the England innings ended shortly before half-past eleven on the second day for 425, it is interesting to observe in the light of the present Test restriction to only 90 overs per day that Australia had bowled 128.4 overs in the England innings. Australia's formidable opening pair of the Victorians Woodfull and Ponsford began their reply before an audience of 31,000 with the gates having been closed. Not until half-past three were they separated with the score at 162, when Ponsford was caught at slip by Hammond off White for 81. This came immediately after the teams had been introduced to His Majesty George V, and led to his being termed England's best change bowler. Incidentally, other distinguished visitors on this

Saturday were HRH the Duke of York, Prince Arthur of Connaught, the Prime Minister Ramsay MacDonald, and Stanley Baldwin, Leader of the Opposition.

They could not have come on a better day as Bradman then came in to play what in retrospect he always declared was his greatest innings. By the close of play Australia were 404 for two with Bradman 155* after a mere two hours and forty minutes at the crease. The English fielding, inspired by their captain Percy Chapman, never flagged but their only success after Ponsford's departure was the wicket of Woodfull stumped for 155 just before the close. Pelham Warner described bowling at him as being "like throwing stones at the Rock of Gibraltar". Bradman was held to be the quickest batsman on his feet that Warner had ever seen as he made each ball the length he wanted it, being particularly severe on the spinners, Robins and White. The latter, having bowled so economically in Australia on the 1928/29 tour on batsmen's wickets, could find no answer to his variety of strokes and dazzling footwork.

On the third day Bradman carried on where he had left off on the Saturday until he was out for 254, to an astounding one-handed catch at extra-cover by the England captain. The ball scarcely left the ground and Bradman is said to have complained about his bad luck on reaching the dressing room. "Just my luck! The first time I lift the ball I am out." After a partnership with Alan Kippax of 192 in three hours, the score now stood at 585 for 3 but England's ordeal was by no means over. Consistent batting by Kippax, Stan McCabe, Vic Richardson, Bert Oldfield and Alan Fairfax saw Australia reach 729 for 6 before Woodfull took pity on England and declared. This remains Australia's highest-ever score against England and the highest innings in a Test at Lord's.

England therefore required 304 to make Australia bat again. Before the close of play they had lost Hobbs and Woolley with the score standing at 98 for 2. The score slumped to 147 for 5 with the dismissals of Hammond, Duleepsinhji and Hendren. The innings was saved by a courageous effort from the captain. After being missed before he had scored from what should have been an easy catch when Ponsford and Richardson both left it for each other, Chapman proceeded to attack the Australian bowlers, Grimmett in particular, to spectacular effect. His 121, marked by tremendously powerful pulling and driving, contained four 6s and twelve 4s before he was finally dismissed, as we are told, just after swallowing a bluebottle! Thus for the first time in Anglo-Australian Tests both captains made centuries. Strangely enough, after opening bowler Tate's making of the second-highest score in the first innings, the feat was repeated when his opening bowler colleague Allen, making his Test debut with a score of 57, was beaten only by his captain in the second innings.

Australia required only 72 to win but in this absorbing game they were made to struggle for every run. Ponsford, Bradman and Kippax were dismissed with only 22 on the board but the

Duleep
in a pose
reminiscent
of his uncle,
Ranjitsinhji.

CHELTENHAM COLLEGE.

APPLICATION FORM.

This Form is to be filled up and sent to the Bursar as soon as the Parent, or Guardian, has decided to seek admission for a Boy.

INSTRUCTIONS.—All Christian Names to be written at full length. The Blank Spaces to be carefully and fully filled up.

Dated the *18th* day of *October* 19 *19*

Pupil's { Surname *Duleepsinhji*
{ ~~Christian~~ Names *Kumar Shri*

Born on the *20th* day of *June* 19 *06*

Father's { Name in full
{ Profession   Nationality
{ and Address (if living)

If no Father
Surviving Parent or   Name   *R.S. Goodchild*
Guardian's   Address   *Wellesley Latham Road*
                                                                        Cambridge

When Pupil will join the College   *January 1920*

In which Department—Senior (over 13)
                    or Junior (under 13) :

In which Side, A Classical, or B Military and
Engineering, or C Modern ? *(see over page)*   *Engineering*

In which Master's House (or with what
relation) will he reside ?

(The House Master should be communicated with direct in the event of his being desired to send the boy to any particular House.)

For what Profession is he destined ?   *Engineer, as far as we can tell*

Give Names and Addresses of the
Schoolmasters or Private Tutors
with whom he has been for the
last three years, with the dates   *H. Lomas Eq. St Faiths Cambridge*
                                                           via May 1919

NOTE.—Notice of the intention to withdraw a Pupil must be given, in writing, to the Bursar not later than the First Day of the Term at the end of which the Pupil is to be withdrawn, and in the case of a Boarder a like notice to the Master of the Boarding House, in default of which payment of the full fees for the Term next ensuing will be charged.

On the above-named Pupil being admitted to the College I agree that he shall be subject to all the Rules and Regulations of the College for the time being as sanctioned by the College Authorities, and that I will, in all matters relating to the said Pupil's connection with the College, be subject to the said Rules and Regulations.

Signature of Parent, or Guardian,

R.S. Goodchild

Application form for Cheltenham College 1919. Notice the inaccurate date of birth - should be 13th June 1905.

Top: Undergraduate, Clare College, Cambridge University, 1924-25. Duleep is third from the left on the second row. Below: Cheltenham College's "Red Book" entry form. His cousin's name appears at the bottom of the page.

R E D   B O O K.

Name	Form	House	Date of Birth	Entered	placed
Caulfeild F.StG. Sn Vl, (11) (6)		Jones	Oct 7 1903 Entered Senior	Sept 1916 Sept 1917	H S Jr H V H
Laurie E.F.	H V.2.11	Jones	Sep 8 1903 Entered Senior	May 1916 Jan 1918	L1V Jan L 1Vb .il
Penn T. C.	LV H.	Jones	Sep 3 1904	Jan 1919	4 H.
Pulcepsinhji	3 H.	Jones	Jun 20 1906	Jan 1920	3 H
~~Chojlotel J~~	3b Jun		*Sep' '18*		
Ramsinghji	3 H.	Jones	~~July 2~~ 1905	Jan 1920	3 H

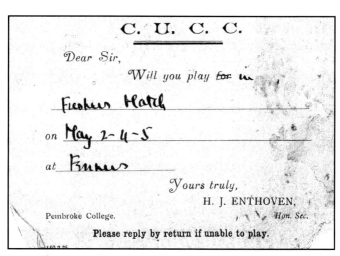

C. U. C. C.

Dear Sir,

Will you play for in

Fresher Match

on May 2-4-5

at Fenners

Yours truly,

H. J. ENTHOVEN,

Pembroke College.

Hon. Sec.

Please reply by return if unable to play.

Top: From such modest beginnings! Duleep's invitation to play in the Freshers' Match at Cambridge 1925.
Below: Cambridge University team 1928 with five future England players - and the father-in-law of a future England captain!
Back row: ED Blundell, JT Morgan, MJC Allom, EF Longrigg. Middle Row : RWV Robins, MJ Turnbull, FJ Seabrook (Captain), KS Duleepsinhji, TC Longfield. Front Row : ET Killick, NG Wykes.

Duleep poses in front of the scoreboard at
Fenner's after his record score for the
university against Middlesex in 1927.

Top: Clare College team in 1925.
Below: Cambridge University v The
Australians in 1926 at Fenner's. Three
future England players on the Cambridge
side: Duleep, RWV Robins (on ground front
left) MJ Turnbull (middle row, extreme left)
and Duleep. The Australian side, captained
by HL Collins, included such greats
as CG Macartney, W Bardsley,
WM Woodfull, WH Ponsford, CV Grimmett,
AA Mailey and J Ryder.

Two "immortals" of Sussex take the field,
Maurice Tate and Duleep.

TELEGRAMS,
LORD'S GROUND LONDON.
TELEPHONE Nº
PADDINGTON 0144 (PAVILION.)
PADDINGTON 5884 (PAVILION)
PADDINGTON 3131 (TENNIS COURT.)
PADDINGTON 4675 (HOTEL)

June 11 1929

Lord's Cricket Ground,
London, N.W. 8.

My dear Duleep!
The Selection
Committee will be very pleased
if you will play for
England v. South Africa
at Birmingham on June
15th. I enclose form
he Board of Control. has
asked me to send out.
I have booked a room
at Queen's Hotel
Shrimp &c

**Duleep's rather informal invitation from
Chairman of Selectors, HDG Leveson
Gower, "Shrimp", to make his Test debut
at Edgbaston in 1929.**

2d.   SUSSEX COUNTY CRICKET GROUND, HOVE.   **2d.**

May 7, 8 & 9, 1930.   SUSSEX v. NORTHANTS. Sussex won the Toss.

Play starts at 11.30 each day.   Lunch at 1.30.   Draw at 6.30.

SUSSEX	First Innings	Second Innings
1 Bowley, E. H.	c Bellamy b Thomas 1	
2 Parks, J.	c Liddell b Thomas 9	
3 K. S. Duleepsinhji	st Bellamy b Matthews 333	
4 Parks, H.	b Clark 11	
5 Langridge, J.	b Cox 17	
6 Cook, T.	c Liddell b Clark 19	
7 Wensley, A.	run out 0	
8 A. H. H. Gilligan (Cpt.)	not out 8	
9 Tate, M. W.	b Partridge 111	
*10 Cornford, W.		
11 Hollingdale, R. A.		

b.   l.b. 6   w.   n.b. 6   12 b.   l.b.   w.   n.b.
Total **521** dec for 7 wkts   Total —

Runs at fall { 1- 1   2- 30   3- 107   4- 182   5- 236   6- 490   7- 514   8-   9-   10-
of wicket { 1-   2-   3-   4-   5-   6-   7-   8-   9-   10-

Bowling Analysis.	o.	m.	r.	w.	wd.	n.b.	o.	m.	r.	w.	wd.	n.b.
Clark	27	1	75	2			20	16	0			
Thomas	29	11	69	2			3	0	26	0		
Partridge	12	0	80	1								
Matthews	22	2	101	1								
Jupp	20	3	92	0								
Cox	11	2	50	1								

NORTHANTS	First Innings	Second Innings
1 Woolley, C.	b Wensley 1 8 c Duleep b Wensley 4	
2 Bakewell, A.	c ... b Parks 12 b Tate 7	
3 Timms, J. E.	c Parks b Langridge 19 lbw b Tate 20	
4 V. C. W. Jupp (Cpt.)	c Richards b Langridge 6 c Cox b Tate 11	
5 Matthews, A.	lbw b Parks 13 c Duleep b Tate 0	
*6 Bellamy, B.	b ... 21 c Cornford b Tate 35	
7 Liddell, A.	c Gilligan b Bowley 18 c Cook b Tate 28	
8 Cox, A.	run out b Tate 40 c Cornford b Cook 4	
9 Thomas, A.	c ... b Langridge 29 b Hollingdale 11	
10 Partridge, R.	not out b Tate 2	
11 Clark, E.	b Tate not out 0	

b. 9   l.b. 4   w.   n.b.   13 b. 2   l.b. 1   w.   n.b.   3
Total — **187**   Total   125

Runs at fall { 1- 28   2- 32   3- 32   4-   5- 70   6- 84   6- 102   7- 113   8- 175   9- 183   10- 187
of wicket { 1- 13   2- 13   3- 44   4- 45   5- 45   6- 97   7- 106   8- 119   9- 124   10- 125

Bowling Analysis.	o.	m.	r.	w.	wd.	n.b.	o.	m.	r.	w.	wd.	n.b.
Tate	9.5	1	18	2			20.2	3	45	7		
Wensley	28	10	65	4			14	5	41	1		
Parks	22	14	37	2	b ...		2	0	12	0		
Langridge	16	7	31	1			1	0	4	1		
Hollingdale	10	2	21	0			8	3	14	1		
Bowley	13	4	32	1			4	2	8	0		

* Wicket Keeper.   Umpires—Toone & Chester   Scorers—E. Killick & E. Bullimer

Next Match on this Ground—May 24, 26, 27, SUSSEX v. SOMERSET

Printed on the Ground by H. CROWHURST, Printer to the S.C.C.C., 50-1-2, Market Street, Brighton.

Sussex won by an innings & 209 runs

A member's scorecard recording Duleep's then record score for Sussex, not beaten until 2003 by Murray Goodwin.

The press acclaims Duleep's 173 v Australia at Lord's on his "Ashes" debut.

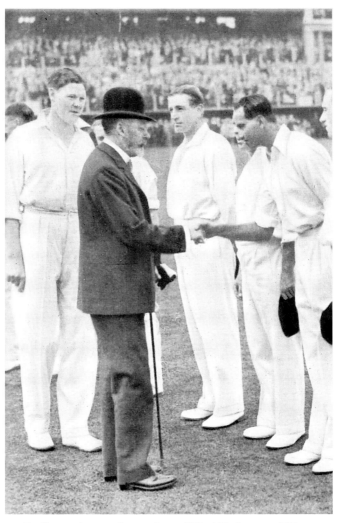

Duleep introduced to His Majesty, King George V, by England captain Percy Chapman at Lord's in 1930.

Top : The glory of Duleep's game,
the exquisite late-cut.
Below : Sussex County Cricket Club
1932, in what was to be Duleep's last season.
Back Row : John Langridge, HE Hammond,
James Langridge, HW Parks.
Front Row : TEF Cook, MW Tate, AER
Gilligan, KS Duleepsinhji (Captain), EH
Bowley, AF Wensley, W Cornford.

TELEGRAMS,
LORD'S GROUND, LONDON.
TELEPHONE N^{os}
ABERCORN 1446 (PAVILION)
ABERCORN 1613 (PAVILION)
ABERCORN 1838 (TENNIS COURT)
ABERCORN 4675 (HOTEL)

Lord's Cricket Ground,
London, N.W. 8.

6th August, 1932.

Dear *Duleep*.

        I send you herewith a provisional list of
fixtures for the forthcoming M.C.C. Australasian tour.

        E.C.Devereux, Hosier, High Street, Eton, will,
on application, forward to you a blazer, two caps and two ties.
He has been given instructions to make one cap with a big peak.
The other cap will be made according to your instructions. You
should advise him as to whether you wish your blazer to be lined,
and of course give him all measurements.

        Will you please send me as soon as possible your
dentist's certificate? I am assuming that all is satisfactory
in this respect.

        As I think you already know, the S.S."Orontes"
leaves London on Saturday, September 17th. There will be a
dinner at Lord's at 7 p.m. on Friday, September 16th, when the
M.C.C. Committee will wish you good luck, so please arrange to
be present. (Morning Dress.)

        Mr.Palairet will be writing to you later on in
regard to other matters.

        You should arrange to have the M.C.C. touring
colours painted on all your luggage. Small samples of the colours
will be forwarded to you by Mr.Palairet.

        Will all good wishes,

        Yours sincerely,

(Enc.)

        W. Findlay

        Sec., M.C.C.

K.S.Duleepsinhji,
    C/o Sussex County Cricket Club,
        County Ground,
            HOVE.

**MCC Secretary, William Findlay, informs
Duleep of the arrangements for the 1932-33
tour of Australia. Unfortunately
he was too ill to go.**

Top: Duleep relaxes after one
of his centuries.
Below: As Indian High Commissioner in
Australia, Duleep with his wife chats with
Robert Menzies, the Australian
Prime Minister.

Duleep back home in India.

KUMAR SHRI DULEEPSINHJI
1905~1959

**Cambridge University, Sussex and England
- from a portrait by Leonie Smith.**

veteran Woodfull and the nineteen-year-old Stan McCabe held firm against Robins, "spinning the ball tremendously", and Tate, "dead on the spot". Bradman was again dismissed by a sensational catch by Chapman, this time from a hard cut to backward point. According to the legendary cricket writer Neville Cardus, he asked the playwright and novelist Sir James Barrie in amazement if he had seen the catch. Sir James wondered if the ball now in Chapman's hand was the same one which had left Bradman's bat with such velocity! In this truly absorbing game no fewer than 505.4 overs were bowled in less than four days. Again, one must ask if the Test match cricketing public of today is given poor value with only 90 overs a day.

This Test also saw the appearance over Lord's of the doomed airship R101. Later in the year it crashed near Beauvais in France, killing forty-four people including the Secretary of Air, Lord Thomson.

After falling cheaply in each innings to that master of left-arm spin Charlie Parker, in the Gloucestershire match at Gloucester which immediately followed the Test, Duleep ran into form in time for the third Test at Headingley with 67 in a thrilling match at Folkestone with Kent. After being well behind on the first innings, Sussex won by two wickets with a partnership of 105 with Harry Parks in under an hour being a crucial factor.

The Test was notable, of course, for Don Bradman's 334 following his 254 at Lord's. Seldom can there have been such domination of an attack as that shown by him this season, although he must have come very close to it on many other occasions! In reply Duleep played "superbly" for 35 before being bowled by an "unplayable" delivery from Hornibrook. Hammond's 113 was not enough to save the follow-on, but England were rescued by bad light, Duleep in the Stygian gloom being dismissed once again by Hornibrook.

Immediately following this game Duleep enjoyed his third triumph of the season at Lord's by scoring a century in each innings for the Gentlemen v the Players. The only batsmen to score two separate hundreds in this fixture previously had been RE Foster for the Gentlemen and JH King for the players; moreover, Duleep's feat of scoring two centuries in a match twice in the same season had previously only been accomplished by Foster, Tom Hayward and Jack Hobbs. In this rain-spoiled fixture he played a masterly first innings of 125 in just over two and a half hours, out of a disappointing score of 292. The star bowler for the Players was that Yorkshireman so renowned for his batting, Maurice Leyland. His left-arm spin earned him figures of 7-94 and makes one wonder just how good a bowler he may have been had there not been such great left-arm bowlers in his county side as Wilfred Rhodes, Roy Kilner and Hedley Verity.

In the second innings Duleep's score of 103* was made out of 179 in two hours and five minutes. The feature of his play was "admirably timed and powerful driving, "although there were strokes all round the wicket to savour. To hasten the declaration he and GOB Allen added 94 in thirty-five minutes. He could not have made this second innings century had it not been for RES Wyatt's sacrificing of his own wicket to a run-out when in fact it was Duleep who was at fault. After being well beaten by the first ball of a Freeman over he then proceeded to hit the next three for scorching boundaries. The return of Leyland into the attack to try to repeat his first innings success led to two mighty sixes over Sutcliffe's head at long-off.

From Lord's came the short trip to Hove with Essex as the visitors. Sussex finished 152 behind on the first innings with Duleep bowled by Nichols for 0. Essex batted again, leaving the home side 432 to win! They finished on 302 for 3 with the young Indian at his most sparkling with 185* scored in a mere three and a half hours and containing one of the biggest sixes ever seen on the ground. He dominated a partnership of 291 for the second wicket with Ted Bowley who was eventually out for a well-earned fifty. "First-class all the time whether on defence or attack. All his better-known strokes were used - the late chop cut, his drive off the body past point or through the covers and the well-placed strokes to leg and between square-leg and mid-on."

This was an excellent preparation for the fourth Test at Old Trafford at the end of July. Alas, the notorious Manchester weather did its worst again and there was play for only forty-five minutes in total on the last two days of the allotted four days. After Australia's 345, with

Duleep catching Bradman smartly at slip off the bowling of the young Scottish-born leg-spinner Ian Peebles for a mere 14, there was only enough time left for England to reply with 251 for 8. In an innings of 54, however, his class was again apparent in his "gem of an innings". Grimmett was played in exemplary fashion with Duleep's footwork in driving and cutting being of the highest order.

The lack of play on the final day at Old Trafford did at least mean that Maurice Tate and Duleep were relatively fresh to start the following day at Portsmouth after a long journey. After being seemingly in an impregnable position Sussex almost lost against Hampshire. The visitors scored 400 for 8 declared with Duleep scoring 188, his ninth century of the season, in the course of which he became the first English county player to score 2,000 runs in a season - Bradman had preceded him for the Australians. His innings "occasioned much delight" as, scoring freely to all parts of the ground, he and Bowley added 230 in two hours and twenty minutes. Hampshire were made to follow on and, making something of a recovery in the second innings, they still only left Sussex to make 102 to win. However, in the end Sussex were hanging on at 77 for 7 with Duleep's 28 being the top score.

Before the final Test at the Oval, there followed a lean spell during which he scored only 31 runs in four innings. Percy Chapman was replaced as captain by Bob Wyatt of Warwickshire who won the toss and elected to bat. England's score of 405 was respectable, but not likely to stretch

Australia too much with the "Don" in such incredible form, and so it proved. Duleep's contribution was a delightful innings of 50 scored out of 65 in fifty minutes. His stroke-play was outstanding after what had been rather a dour start to the day as he attacked the Australian bowlers with "driving, hooking and cutting in dazzling style". The trouble was, however, that in the context of a "timeless" Test to decide the outcome of the Ashes, the series standing at one-all, he should not have got out to a careless shot. He had the attack at his mercy when he played a poor stroke to be caught off Grimmett. Australia replied with 695, Don Bradman 232 to set up a record 974 runs in a series, causing England to follow on. Duleep had achieved an excellent reputation as a slip-fielder but in this long innings, when called upon to field away from the wicket, he received accolades for his work in the deep. His speed over the ground, picking up and strong, accurate throwing were a major feature of England's out-cricket. Going in to bat on what was the sixth day of the Test, the fifth having been washed out, Duleep played another beautiful but relatively brief innings before falling yet again to Hornibrook, the left-arm spinner, for 46. Australia duly won by an innings and 39 runs.

Although Australia had regained the Ashes, at least Duleep had had a successful series against them, finishing second in aggregate and average to Herbert Sutcliffe with 416 runs at 59.42.

The rest of the season was something of an anti-climax as although playing several useful innings, he never reached more than 58 in eight further visits to the wicket, in three of which he again fell to the wiles of the Australian Hornibrook. It is possible that this lack of form could be attributed to a complete lack of recovery from his chest problems and consequent fatigue after a long season. In spite of this disappointing end of season, he did, however, score most runs by a county player - 2,562 - and was second to Sutcliffe in the averages with 56.93. His nine centuries were second only to Bradman's ten who, by the way, scored 2,960 runs at an average of 98.66! Duleep was clearly one of England's brightest hopes for the future.

His batting achievements during the summer led to his receiving an enormous number of telegrams and letters, somewhere in the region of 200. These came particularly after his 333 against Northamptonshire and his 173 in the Lord's Test. A friend of his called Guy, referring to the fiery left-arm pace bowler, conjectured: "I suppose Clark tried bowling at your head!" Jim Seabrook, an Old Cheltonian, wrote from Radley College to "My dear Smith" on May 5 after Duleep's 333: " You're playing while I am slogging away teaching the young... I am writing this while the lads are doing prep." The great Cambridge University, Gloucestershire and England cricketer, Gilbert Jessop, notable for his extraordinary hitting, sent him a telegram from Edgware Golf Club. "Hearty congratulations on your magnificent knock. Hope you will repeat similar figures in the Test Match." Jessop was able to congratulate Duleep on the Friday of the Lord's Test from his address in 3 Sunnydale

Gardens: "Well played. My prophecy came true. Hearty congratulations and regards to your uncle." Colin, from The Grand Hotel, Eastbourne, wrote of his splendid innings at Lord's "which has helped to put England in a winning position". George Bonas, Honorary Secretary of the Irish Cricket Union, sent him his congratulations addressed to "Your Royal Highness".

It had truly been an extraordinary season. At the age of 25 Duleep surely stood on the threshold of even greater achievements.

7.

CAPTAIN OF SUSSEX

AFTER HIS MAINLY triumphant season of 1930 Duleepsinhji spent a further winter in the south of France and skiing in Switzerland to fight against his pulmonary problems. The MCC sent a touring side to South Africa that winter under the captaincy of Percy Chapman, a side of which Duleep would surely have been asked to be a member. It is perhaps a moot point whether or not he was omitted for political reasons, as was D'Oliveira originally some thirty-eight years later, or whether he genuinely decided that further recuperation was necessary. Whilst in Switzerland he was invited by the Sussex committee to take over the captaincy from Harold Gilligan who was finding the pressures of business too much to continue. In this respect he beat Ranji who was twenty-seven before being appointed, whereas Duleep was a mere twenty-five.

At the beginning of the 1931 season *The Cricketer* singled him out as "This Week's Personality" and dedicated a whole page to his achievements of 1924-1930. The author stated that he had some claims to be considered the finest batsman in England "at the present time". This is some statement when we remember that amongst his contemporaries were people such as

Wally Hammond, Herbert Sutcliffe and Patsy Hendren to name but three. The article goes on to describe him as having been the finest schoolboy batsman of his generation and lists his strengths as being "naturally gifted with exceptionally keen eyesight and quickness of foot, he combines these with an aggressive style and practically all the strokes, his leg-glancing, being, as one might expect, particularly delightful". His all-round fielding ability is commented upon, particularly in the slips, and there is the hope that he would be able to tour Australia in 1932/33 to be a response to Bradman's high scoring. This was a most flattering thought, but alas, as we saw in the first chapter, ill-health caused his withdrawal from the touring party. He also features in the same edition of the magazine of May 9, 1931, in an article by Sir Home Gordon, Bart., entitled *Brains*. The author cites as examples of brains in fielding two catches made by Duleep which showed extraordinary anticipation: one was in New Zealand when he took a slip-catch by moving from second slip position to fourth whilst the ball was being bowled, and the other was when he caught the Australian, Clarrie Grimmett, almost at his side when playing a "safe" defensive stroke.

Although playing in all three Tests against the visiting New Zealanders, Duleep was able to play in ten more county matches than in 1930 and as that great bowler Maurice Tate was also able to do the same, Sussex rose from seventh to fourth in the championship. Both men easily headed the respective batting and bowling averages.

The season of 1931 was notable even by English standards for being very wet, but there were several notable achievements for Duleep both in his own performances and in the side's improvement. After a very poor start in which at one stage they slipped to thirteenth, the county finished three places higher than in 1930 and Duleep himself scored no fewer than twelve centuries. By mid-June Sussex had won only one out of nine championship games, whilst the captain's form was most inconsistent. He had batted superbly at Old Trafford in early May for his 69 in the second innings when Sussex won by four wickets against Lancashire, the reigning champions, in a low-scoring game. His first big innings, however, did not come until a fortnight later when he scored 162 against Surrey at the Oval, taking part in a 250 partnership with Ted Bowley made in three hours. His off-driving and late-cutting were particularly memorable. In his 112 at Northampton he "played delightful cricket", whilst in his chanceless 112 at Leicester in early June he "played with refreshing freedom". In three other matches he had, however, been dismissed for single figures in each innings, falling twice at Lord's to the FJ Durston/GOB Allen combination and twice at Chesterfield to the wiles of leg-spinner TB Mitchell, aided and abetted by wicketkeeper H Elliott.

From mid-June, however, Sussex proceeded to win ten of the next eleven matches in which he played, including a non-championship fixture with Notts and a game with Cambridge University. They rose to fourth position with the captain in awesome form. He scarcely failed and twice within this period came very close to scoring a century in each innings, a feat he had achieved twice in the previous season and once in 1929. The Staples brothers dismissed him for 97 and 109 for Notts at Horsham and Kent at Tunbridge Wells narrowly missed the repetition of his 1929 performance against them as this time he "only" scored 91 and 127. The second innings was a particularly memorable one as after his 91 in "faultless style" on the second day, Sussex had to score 314 to win on a wearing wicket against Freeman, who had taken eight wickets in the first innings. This Sussex proceeded to do with three hours of brilliant batting. Duleep scored his runs in well under two hours and was well assisted by Ted Bowley's invaluable rapid 78. His 140 at Chelmsford was a significant factor in his county's ten-wicket victory over Essex, although much of his thunder was stolen by Harry Parks whose 200* was to be his highest-ever career score. Just over two weeks later in the return fixture with Essex at Hove, Duleep's 133 was a major contribution to Sussex's win by an innings and 63 runs. He took part in a second-wicket partnership of 237 in just over two hours with Ted Bowley (137) characterised by "refreshingly varied hitting, their accuracy of stroke was remarkable".

The Worcestershire match at Dudley starting on July 25 saw him make the first of four consecutive hundreds. His 161* out of a total of 361 for 3 declared was scored in three and a half hours with his usual array of "delightful and well-varied strokes." The home county, managing only

96 and 132 in reply, lost by an innings and 133 runs, the Sussex bowling hero being James Langridge, who followed his 67* with figures of 6-15 and 4-34 with his left-arm spinners. He then proceeded to score 109 in the Oval Test with New Zealand, more of which anon, before returning to the county side at Hove. Here he scored 103, his tenth century of the season, in the home side's nine wicket victory when James Langridge again took ten wickets in the match. His fourth three-figure score in this wonderful spell came in the following match with Hampshire at Hastings with 127 during his stay of two and three-quarter hours. Showing his best form, he scored with ease all round the wicket and made his runs "with delightful certainty" against an impressive attack, particularly Alec Kennedy. Although Hampshire were forced to follow on, there had been too much play lost to rain to force a victory.

After this wonderful spell his form tailed off somewhat as he managed only one more century in a season when he appeared to be a serious contender for overtaking the record of sixteen centuries in a season, scored by Jack Hobbs in 1925. His 103 was scored at Hove for Sussex when he "batted most attractively for two hours" against the touring New Zealanders. Included in his moderate end-of-season performances was a double failure of 5 and 2 in the Yorkshire match at Hove against that up-and-coming great bowler Hedley Verity.

As stated earlier, Duleep played in all three Tests against New Zealand. As a virtually untried Test nation they were originally only granted the one

Test at Lord's in late June; however, they put up such a splendid performance in this game that the authorities allowed them two more Tests at the Oval and Old Trafford to take the place of fixtures with Surrey and Lancashire respectively. Duleep was out cheaply in each innings at Lord's but was in splendid form at the Oval when he scored 109 in England's victory by an innings and 26 runs. Playing in his customary dazzling manner, he added 178 with Herbert Sutcliffe in two and a quarter hours, his on-side play being particularly outstanding. The final Test at Old Trafford was all too predictable with no play being possible until after three o'clock on the last afternoon. There was time, however, for Duleep and Sutcliffe to share another large stand of 126 in just under two hours. Duleep was finally dismissed for 63, whilst the Yorkshireman went on to yet another century. Duleep's innings at the Oval and Old Trafford had been entirely in the company of Sutcliffe.

If he had a weakness at this stage one would draw attention to his facing left-arm spinners. His dismissals by Hornibrook of Australia in the 1930 season and by Verity at Hove have already been remarked upon. It is evident that the New Zealand captain, TC Lowry, called upon his young left-armers Allcott and Vivian as soon as Duleep arrived at the crease and although they did have some success against him, he still achieved an average of 52.00 in the Tests.

In spite of his disappointing climax to the season, he finished with 2,684 runs for the campaign with twelve centuries and an average of 54.77. It had been a wonderful season for him and as the older members said, reminiscent of his uncle at the turn of the century. His career average was now only fractionally under 50 and, as in 1930, he was the first to reach 2,000 runs, an aggregate he had now achieved in three consecutive seasons. For Sussex alone his aggregate of 1,859 runs was more than 500 better than his nearest competitor with his average being twenty greater than the next man's. Duleep was the first amateur since CB Fry in 1903-05 to score over 2,500 runs in three consecutive seasons. He now seemed to be approaching the very height of his powers and, as he was only 26, the cricket world had much to look forward to.

In addition, his captaincy of the Sussex side had proved inspirational, "unobtrusive, sympathetic and masterly", which led to many letters of congratulation, prominent amongst these being those from Henry Thirkill, a tutor at Duleep's Cambridge college, Clare, and Mr WL Knowles, the highly-regarded secretary of the county club. Perhaps the most memorable of these letters was that written by Sir Home Gordon, Bart.

UNION CLUB,
BRIGHTON.

14 SEPT 1931

My dear Duleep,

When we meet at dinner on Thursday I may not have a chance of a private word with you.

Therefore I am writing to tell you how much I appreciate your friendship and charm to me. It is to you that I owe the greater part of the pleasure of the past season.

Your batting has been a delight and is growing in reliability without losing any distinction in brilliance.

But it is on your captaincy that I particularly want to congratulate you. Perhaps no one, not even Harold, appreciates what a curiously difficult emotional team Sussex is to captain. You had to feel your way and you have come through as an admirable individualistic observant leader. Your talk to them at Taunton did them a lot of good. They will all follow you with enthusiasm and confidently I expect even better results next summer especially if you can be at the April practices.

My warmest felicitations and all best wishes.
Ever your sympathetic and sincere friend,

Home Gordon

Home Gordon was correct in his forecast that Sussex would have even better results the following season, but he could never have realised that Duleep's inspired leadership and batting skills would be seen no more after the Somerset match at Taunton in mid-August.

He was invited in a letter addressed to HH Prince KR (sic) Duleepsinhji to be a vice-president of Westbourne Park Cricket Club, respectability being given to the offer by the assurance that Arthur Gilligan was one already! Lanka Nanda Cricket club in Ceylon, also addressing him as HH

Prince, were anxious to have his acceptance of an offer to become Patron: "May it please your Highness..."

In the English winter of 1931/32 Duleep returned to India to spend some time with his uncle who had not been very well during his stay in Europe in 1932. India were preparing for their first Test trip to England and their board eagerly sought his advice in selecting the team because of his great experience in county and Test cricket. He was co-opted onto the Selection Committee after having turned down the possibility of captaining the side himself. He is credited with having seen the exciting possibilities of Amar Singh who came from Rajkot where Duleep had attended college. Amar Singh was selected for the 1932 side and made a great reputation as a fine bowler and more than useful batsman. He took 111 wickets on the tour at 20.78 with five or more wickets in an innings on no fewer than nine occasions and scored centuries against Lancashire and HDG Leveson Gower's XI. In India's inaugural Test at Lord's he claimed the prized wickets of Hammond and Ames, both bowled, and Sutcliffe caught. He also toured England with the 1936 side, his most memorable performance being 6 for 35 in the first innings of the Lord's Test, including the first five in the batting order. This fine cricketer, discovered by Duleep, died at the tragically early age of 29.

Duleep's efforts as a selector were acknowledged in a letter from the Board of Control for Cricket in India dated February 6 1932, signed by President Grant Govan:

K.S. *Duleep Sinhji,*
Jamnagar.

Dear Sir,

I am directed by the Board of Control for Cricket in India to convey to you copy of the resolution given below and to express to you the very grateful thanks of the Board for all your help in connection with the work of the Selection Committee.

Yours faithfully,
Grant Govan (signature)
President.

Copy of the Resolution

"The Board resolved to place on record their appreciation of the excellent work done by the Selection Committee in selecting the Team to proceed to England in 1932. The Members of the Selection Committee, namely Mr AL Hosie, the Maharaj Kumar of Vizianagram, Kumar Shree Ghanshyem Sinhji and Mr Ahsan-ul-Haq together with the assistance of His Highness the Maharajah of Patiala and Raj Kumar Duleep Sinhji as co-opted members, have given freely of their time to the arduous work of selecting the Team from among cricketers spread over the whole of India and the Board wish to congratulate the Members of the

Selection Committee on the successful conclusion of their work. The Board desire especially to thank Raj Kumar Duleep Sinhji who has given up a large proportion of his short time in India to this work in the interest of cricket in India."

Duleep played just one match whilst in his homeland when he played for the Viceroy's XII against the Roshanara Club XII. This game was played as one of the trials for selecting the 1932 India side to tour England and it was thought that the inclusion of Duleep and the Nawab of Pataudi, then playing for Worcestershire, would add extra competition for the aspiring bowlers. This certainly happened in the second innings when they shared a stand of 189 with Duleep making 173 in his customary elegant style in the presence of his uncle.

Whilst in India he was sent a cable by Mr WL Knowles, his county secretary, to offer him the captaincy again for the 1932 season, this decision being a unanimous one of the Sussex committee and was to take effect from the second week in April.

8.

IMMEDIATE AFTERMATH OF THE 1932 SEASON

AS WE HAVE SEEN in an earlier chapter, Duleep was forced to give up any thoughts of cricket in the immediate future at the end of the 1932 season after his collapse at Taunton. For a few weeks he led a hermit-like existence as the only guest in a hotel on Bodmin Moor. He then was forced to return to the Montana clinic in Switzerland for further treatment whilst Jardine's team, of which he should have been a member, was battling it out in Australia. He decided that when he felt a little fitter he would go to help his brother Raj Kumar Digvigaysinhji in India.

Sussex had not given up hope for his return and on January 12, 1933 he received a letter from the Sussex Secretary Mr WL Knowles (author's own italics):

> *"Am delighted to hear good news of your health. Would you be willing to be captain just in August when all matches are at home?*
>
> *You would be officially club captain as your name as skipper goes such a long way."*

Robert Scott would agree to be vice-captain and carry on until August.

115

On February 28 Duleep received two missives, one typed and one hand-written, both from Mr Knowles. The typed message informed Duleep that at a committee meeting on the 27th of the month he had been unanimously re-elected as captain for the county club for 1933. The hand-written letter, of a more personal nature, repeated the point he had made to Duleep in his communication of January 12: "If you will allow your name to remain as skipper it will be of great service in keeping people interested in the county club." Any fears that Duleep had at Scott's alarm at taking his place and respect from the team were ill-founded as "knowing these lads as I do (that) is absurd".

There can be no clearer indication of the standing and popularity which Duleep enjoyed with the club than these efforts from the secretary to keep him on board.

He received a letter from Arthur Gilligan, his mentor, which is interesting for its period language: " ....how beastly sorry I am to hear of your illness. I am ever so sorry, old chap." Perhaps we had better not follow too closely the next paragraph as he continues, "Dick Lowe was feeling sorry as the little waitress had gone from the Royal York but I hear she's at the Grosvenor Hotel, so must pop in to see her."

He also received an invitation in this period on February 16 from a Mr FD Mills, Hon. Secretary of the Sussex Ramblers Cricket Club, to be their President. How even further we were from a classless society in those pre-war days can be seen in an extract from the invitation: "I pointed out to you that nearly all the members were old Varsity and Public School men and members of the Sussex County" - apparently, no plebs allowed!

Although Duleep was unable to take part personally in the infamous tour of Australia, the Editor of a leading Sunday newspaper thought it would be a good idea if he were to give his impressions of the Tests from his bed at the Montana sanatorium. This would keep the name of Duleep in front of his legions of admirers and, incidentally, would not do much harm to the circulation of the paper! It seemed to be a difficult process, with reports being provided for him in Switzerland by a newspaper representative and then Duleep having to comment on these reports compiled by other commentators. They would probably have added their own opinions which may have complicated matters. However, whatever the mechanics, Duleep readily agreed to do this after insisting it be made known that he would not be receiving any payment. "It will help to pass my time and I will be able to make the article interesting enough for the public to enjoy it."

After the first Test at Sydney which England won by ten wickets, requiring one run to win, Duleep telephoned the London office praising the England side on its magnificent performance, but adding sadly "...it almost breaks my heart not to out there with them all". He continued: "I congratulate Jardine and all of them from the bottom of my heart. And my fellow-countryman, the Nawab of Pataudi too, who must have batted brilliantly."

It is an amazing fact that Pataudi, following the lead of fellow-Indians Ranjitsinhji and Duleepsinhji, also scored a century in his first Test for England against Australia. He failed in the following Test at Melbourne when Bill O'Reilly's greatness was first experienced by England in a ten-wicket haul. Although he was the most successful batsman overall on the tour after the two greats, Sutcliffe and Hammond, he was not selected for any further Tests in the series. One reason could be that he scored too slowly, but another theory is that he upset his captain by voicing disquiet over the tactics used. Jardine was not known to brook any opposition. After he had refused to field in the leg-trap, Jardine banished him to the fine-leg boundary with the taunt of "I see His Highness is a conscientious objector." On a later occasion Pataudi is reported to have said that although Jardine was said to have many fine qualities, "I've been on tour with him for many months and I have yet to come across one." He played one further Test for England against Australia in 1934, but, unlike Ranji and Duleep, he did play eventually for the country of his birth. When normal cricket resumed after the Second World War, he led the Indian touring side of 1946 to England, playing in a further three Tests.

After the loss at Melbourne Duleep's words to *The Star* were ones of encouragement. "There is no need to be depressed... We were caught on a wearing wicket, and it beat us." He went on to say that "Even with the help of the wicket, Australian bowlers gave a very fine performance. O'Reilly must be just the man they are looking for." With great prescience he suggested that Verity, a spin bowler, should replace Bowes for the next Test at Adelaide as there was more potential for turn on that pitch than on any other in Australia. This was in spite of the fact that Bowes had dismissed Bradman first ball for one of the most famous "ducks" of his career - his last Test at the Oval notwithstanding. The Test at Adelaide, one of the most unpleasant in history at the height of the "Bodyline" controversy, was won by England by the overwhelming margin of 338 runs. Ironically, seventeen of the available eighteen wickets - Australian wicket-keeper Bert Oldfield was "retired hurt" in the first innings and was "absent hurt" in the second innings after having been felled by an express delivery from Harold Larwood - were taken by fast or fast-medium bowlers. The exception was Hedley Verity who took Bradman's wicket as his first in Anglo-Australian Tests. Verity also played his part with the bat in scoring 45 and 40 and taking part in vital partnerships.

When asked his views in the calm and safety of Switzerland on the subject of England's leg-theory, he replied, "Half the joy of cricket is derived from the element of personal danger involved."

All this was overshadowed for him, however, when the news came to him during England's second Test in New Zealand at Auckland on April 2 that his uncle had died. Whilst much has been written about Duleep's health problems, it has perhaps been overlooked that Ranji was a long-term sufferer from asthma and associated bronchial problems. His death at the early age of 60 came as a great shock to Duleep whose health, after a promising improvement, took a turn for the worse. There seemed now to be no further hopes of a recovery and all impetus was lost for a return to the cricket field.

He was sent a most moving letter from Pelham Warner, the MCC manager in Australia.

...I cannot say how disappointed I was at your not coming to Australia. It was a real blow to me. We missed you sadly both on and off the field and your absence from cricket today is a tragedy. It grieves me to think that, as you say, you may not be playing again.

This I will say: that the game has a grievous loss by your absence but it is as certain as tomorrow's sun that in the pages of cricket history your name will stand forth as a star of the first magnitude. Your name will live for ever and more and also the spirit and manner in which you played cricket. You and your uncle - no greater names in the game.

Yours ever,
Plum.

In December 1933 Duleep authorised a statement from the Wentworth Dormy House Club in Virginia Water to the effect that he was definitely retiring from international cricket. It was felt that he had made a wonderful recovery from his illness and he added that his present intention was to return to India the moment he was fully recovered, which would probably be in about six months' time. The writer of the article announcing this news was of the opinion that this country was about to lose one of the ablest of cricketers and one of the most charming of men. The celebrated essayist and man of letters, EV Lucas, was so moved that he wrote a letter to Duleep on hearing this news in which he said, "..... I am very sorry to hear of your decision. I now don't much care if next summer never comes at all."

9.

RETURN TO INDIA

AT THE END OF 1934, driven by a great sense of duty, Duleep returned to his homeland in order to assist his elder brother Digvijaysinhji who had become the Jam Saheb of Nawanagar on the death of his uncle Ranjitsinhji. He had enjoyed his cricket career enormously, had made thousands of people happy, had forged lifelong friendships on and off the field and had come to love England.

His brother Digvijaysinhji - or to give him his full title, Captain His Highness Maharajah Shri Sir Digvijaysinhji Ranjitsinhji Jadeja, KCSL, Maharajah Jam Saheb of Jadeja - was as conscientious as his uncle when he took over the title in 1933 and in his period of office until 1948 many public works were completed. Prominent amongst these were the Digvijay Woollen Mills, an aerodrome, and the Ranjit Swimming Pool.

However, Duleep felt it was now the time to move on as India was going through a crucial period and he wondered what he could do to help. His background so far had been "merely" in cricket - surely there was something else he could offer! He had always said that he would retire at the age of 30, even if healthy, to offer service to his country. He had loved his time in England playing "the most wonderful game on earth", but he felt that he could no longer enjoy himself playing it whilst his native country was passing through such a momentous period in its history. He wanted to offer his "humble services" to his country as he continually questioned the lack of his experiences outside cricket. He felt that it was high time that he made a contribution to his country's progress. India was to become his permanent home with the possibility of occasional visits to England for health reasons. In addition to helping his brother in the administration of Nawanagar, he naturally wanted to use his great cricketing knowledge, not to say his contacts, in helping the sport to grow in a country so enthusiastic for the game, having recently acquired Test status.

Having already spotted the great potential of Amar Singh who made such a wonderful impression in his sadly curtailed career, Duleep on his return to India found and encouraged a local cricketer by the name of Mulvantrai Himmatlal Mankad. Always known ever after as Vinoo, he became one of the world's greatest all-rounders, a stylish batsman and classical slow left-arm bowler with cunning flight and deceptive spin. He came to England in 1946 with the Nawab of Pataudi's team and was the last tourist to complete the "double" of 1,000 runs and 100 wickets. One of his more famous feats was in the Lord's Test of 1952 when India in an emergency sent for him from his engagement as a professional in the Lancashire League. His response was to score 72 and 184 and bowl 73 overs in England's first innings for five wickets.

Mankad was ever grateful to Duleep for the help he gave him after spotting his potential as a schoolboy and asking him to open the innings for the Jamnagar team. Vinoo had a tendency to back away to balls directed at the leg-stump; however, so much faith did Duleep have in his potential, that he spent hours in the nets having bowlers bowl at his legs. He told the youngster that one day he would play for India and so he did, to the tune of forty-four Tests and the quickest "double" in Test cricket until beaten to that record by Ian Botham.

In the season 1935/36 an unofficial Australian touring side was due to visit India. The official Australian side was due to visit South Africa under the captaincy of Victor Richardson and it was believed by many that sending this "second XI" would help India to make further development in its progress as a cricket nation. In view of the most laudable motives behind this visit, it is astonishing how much opposition there was to it by the Australian Board of Control. They were unhappy that the request from Frank Tarrant had not come directly from the Indian Board of Control and that the team was to be the responsibility of the Maharajah of Patiala who was financing the enterprise. The Australian Board placed several obstacles in front of Tarrant, including denying him the selection of certain players not required for the official team to South Africa, even retired ones such as Bill Woodfull, Bill Ponsford, Alan Kippax, Jack Gregory and Arthur Mailey. "Australia" was not to be used as the team's title and they were to be known as "The

Maharajah of Patiala's Team of Australian Cricketers", whilst the home side were to be known as "The Maharajah of Patiala's XI of All-India." Under no circumstances was there to be any game designated as a Test to be played or one against any team calling itself "All-India". Needless to say, the Indian press had no hesitation in dubbing the games "Australia" v "All-India", rather than the more ponderous titles favoured by the reactionary Australian Board.

The team was assembled by the aforementioned Frank Tarrant, a cricketer with great experience in Australia, England and India. It was rather an elderly group with ex-Australian captain Jack Ryder at the age of 46 as leader. Also in the side were former Test cricketers such as the "Governor General" Charlie Macartney, aged 49, and bowlers Bertie "Dainty" Ironmonger and Ron Oxenham, 48 and 44 respectively. The Indians were to be led by the Maharajah of Patiala. The selection committee, set up for these games and also to pick the Indian Test team for their second tour of England in 1936, consisted of Dr. Kanga, Pataudi, also now back in India from England, and Duleep. The position of Duleep on the selection committee caused him some embarrassment as reports began to circulate that he may return to cricket as the Indian captain. He had no intention of doing this and he was particularly hurt by the innuendo that he had accepted the post of selector with this object in mind.

There were sixteen first-class matches played with the Australians winning nine and losing three. There were also four unofficial internationals - not "Tests"! - at Bombay, Calcutta, Lahore and Madras in a series which finished at two games all.

By this time Duleep was a married man having taken Princess Jayrajkumari of Rajpipla as his bride earlier in the year. However, even married bliss could not save Duleep as he did not see through this period as a selector for on October 29th he had a recurrence of his illness, returned to a nursing home, and was replaced as a selector by the Maharajkumar of Vizianagram - known as "Vizzy" to his friends. In the meantime, his brother, the Jam Saheb of Nawanagar, was unlike his predecessor Ranji in that he was taking a great interest in the state cricket side. He imported the excellent Bert Wensley from Sussex as player-coach and when Duleep had made a recovery he too took part with his old Sussex colleague in guiding the fortunes of Nawanagar. The Sussex influence was such that they won the Ranji Trophy in 1936-37. This was the third year of the competition, Bombay having won the two previous seasons. There was great rejoicing in the land at this feat which gave Duleep so much pleasure.

Duleep's next significant period as a selector was several years later when, coincidentally, another Australian side came to India. This was in 1945-46 at the end of the Second World War when the Australian Services side played a series of matches. They were on their way home after a very successful summer in England, including a drawn series of "Victory Tests" with England. Duleep and India felt that they had many up-and-coming players of Test standard and these matches would be a real test of their strength. Had the Australians not held England over a series of five games in which the home country had called upon such experienced players as Wally Hammond, Len Hutton, Les Ames, Bill Edrich and Doug Wright? They had several fine players in their number including two who were to make their mark in Test cricket: Lindsay Hassett, the captain, whose start in international cricket had been on Australia's 1938 tour of England, and Keith Miller, the up-and-coming all-rounder from Victoria. Hassett became one of Australia's leading batsmen in the post-war years succeeding Don Bradman as captain, whilst Miller, one of the most glamorous of cricketers of all-time, was to become one of his country's greatest-ever all-rounders.

Another prominent member of the side was the controversial figure of the burly Cecil Pepper who made a great reputation for himself in league cricket in England for many years after the war. The careers of Hassett and Miller are well documented but not that of Pepper who deserves some recognition even after all this passage of time. He was a wonderful all-round player, a very powerful batsman and a bowler of leg-breaks, googlies and flippers. He must be one of the best players not to have played Test cricket, but rumour has it that his forthright language on the field upset Bradman!

Pepper, from Forbes in New South Wales, began his first-class career for his native state in the season 1938-39 and, playing until he was called up for military service two years later, made sixteen appearances. In tandem with the great Bill O'Reilly he was a formidable bowler sharing his hatred of the batsman and not adverse to giving them a little "advice"! (There is nothing new in "sledging"!). In season 1939-40 they each dismissed Bradman in the Sheffield Shield game with South Australia. His strong hitting was seen in an innings for his state against Queensland in 1939 when he scored 81, including seven 6s and eight 4s.

He was a great success in the Australian Services side when the cricket-loving Field Marshal Blamey, Australian Commander-in-Chief, used his influence to transfer players such as Hassett, Cheetham and Pepper himself from Far Eastern theatres of war to play in the "Victory Tests". During these games he dismissed such eminent batsmen as Walter Hammond, Len Hutton, Cyril Washbrook, Bill Edrich and Jack Robertson. His hitting was seen to great effect in the first match at Lord's when Australia were set to score 107 in seventy minutes, which they achieved with only a few balls left. Pepper's share was 54*, including a huge six into the Grandstand. In September, playing against HDG Leveson Gower's XI at Scarborough, his 168 included six 6s and eighteen 4s. One of his 6s went into Trafalgar Square, equalling one by "Buns" Thornton many years previously.

After their visit to India the Services played some games in Australia, including one against South Australia and Bradman! Pepper was sure that he had Bradman lbw but when he had his appeal turned down he enquired "gently" of Umpire Scott, " What do you have to do to get him out?" This is said to have spoiled all chances of Pepper's playing for Australia, so he decided to make his living in the Lancashire Leagues. A typical performance of his came for Rochdale at Stockport in the Central Lancashire League in 1946 when in a two-night match at a packed ground he scored 148* with many enormous sixes and then took 9 for 46. Lancashire were rumoured to want him but opening for Stockport were brothers Barry and Nigel Howard, sons of Lancashire Secretary, Major Rupert Howard. The choice language he used against them is said to have deterred Lancashire from offering him a contract! He was also involved in some heated exchanges of views with several spectators.

Although Pepper himself thought that his little contretemps with Bradman ruled out any possibilities of making the Test team, the latter in his book *Farewell to Cricket* published in 1950, refers to him when recalling the Australian Services mini-tour of Australia in the following terms: "Another who showed every sign of being a great player was Cecil Pepper. Unfortunately for Australia, his skill was lost to this country when he decided to throw in his lot with the Lancashire League." Was Pepper a little hasty in feeling that he had irrevocably blotted his copybook?

For a man who had gained such a reputation as a modest and courteous gentleman for most of his life, controversy seemed to follow Duleep in this role as chairman. That dazzling, if erratic, batsman Mushtaq Ali had been in prime form and was an automatic choice for the first international match against the Australians. Just before the match at Bombay he fell ill and sent a letter to the Board explaining his unfitness for the game. Unfortunately the reply did not reach them and India found themselves a man short before play began on the first morning of the game. Various rumours began to circulate about his non-appearance, all of which infuriated Duleep. He and his selection committee reacted by dropping Mushtaq for the next "Test" at Calcutta, a city where he was very popular. This was not a wise move as there was already great political unrest in the area and the omission of Mushtaq inflamed the situation. During the game between East Zone and the Australians, immediately before the international, there had been riots with armed police confronted by students. Even in the midst of all this violence Mushtaq's cause was not forgotten with placards challenging the selectors: "No Mushtaq, no Test". Duleep himself, a figure of idolatry to cricket-loving Indians, was assaulted and compelled to restore the new idol to the side. What would they have made of this in the gentle backwaters of peaceful Hove with the calm English Channel sea-breezes drifting over the deckchairs?!

Another occasion when Duleep's sterner side was seen was when he was enraged by the negative tactics of Vijay Merchant, the Indian captain. Merchant remains one of the greatest of all India's cricketers, a superbly classical batsman, a man with a propensity for high scores and, with a career average of 71.22, stands second only to Bradman. He was probably an even bigger hero than Mushtaq to the Indians, but this does not hide the fact that he was a very negative captain. Merchant hated to lose, with "safety-first" being his motto. In the first "Test" at Bombay he had declared, leaving Australia to score 113 in twenty minutes. Not only that, he then ordered his bowlers to bowl wide of the stumps, all of which caused the furious Duleep to shout at India's greatest cricketer: "Merchant, you have brought shame upon Indian cricket." Again, would the Sussex members and supporters recognise this side of his character? Whether or not it was because he had had this exchange with the great Merchant or not, he was voted off the Indian selection committee which was to choose the 1946 team to come to England. Much behind-the-scene activities, mostly of a political nature, saw the Nawab of Pataudi win the vote for the captaincy over Merchant. Was it a case of a prince being deemed more acceptable than a rich businessman?

10.

FURTHER CONTRIBUTIONS TO INDIAN CRICKET

DULEEP'S CONTRIBUTIONS to Indian cricket were by no means confined solely to his periods as a selector. He was always offering advice to the Indian Board of Control and also earned a reputation for his thoughts on the game "remarkable for their originality and thoughtfulness". There were several principles which he held dearly and never tired of repeating in his conversations, speeches and writings.

One of his particular concerns was the over-doping of wickets in India which led to such high scoring with the consequence of tedious games. He felt it essential that bowlers must be given a chance if the game were to develop and Indian cricket improve. A few of the game's rulers were upset by his campaign, but it is highly likely that the great majority of cricket lovers would see the sense in his views.

Perhaps it may come as a surprise to realise just how passionate Duleep was about coaching to improve the standards of youngsters. One could be excused for thinking that a player of his type, so full of flair, natural ability and artistry, would not concern himself too much with what he called the "grammar" of the game as it had all seemed to come to him so easily. How wrong would one be to have this assumption! His personal attitude to coaching can be seen from these words by England leg-spinner Ian Peebles about Duleep's involvement with Aubrey Faulkner at his school in what must have been the Spring of 1928 after his having missed most of the 1927 season: "KS Duleepsinhji - Smith to his friends - had just recovered from a serious illness, and spent the Spring playing himself back to form in our nets. He was at that stage not only a beautifully fluent batsman of very good technique, but also a model and attentive pupil. Faulkner naturally made no basic alterations to his play, but put forward several suggestions with a view to strengthening various strokes, and correcting minor faults. It was interesting to see how eagerly Duleep received such advice, and how immediately he would apply it, with obvious benefit to the stroke concerned." Faulkner could well have been the model of the ideal coach which Duleep was advocating in his campaigns to revolutionise the game in India as described below.

He held very strong views on the coaching of youngsters and the necessity to find the right kind of people to carry out this essential task. A good coach must be in place for a boy or girl when they are young as the older they become, the more set they may be in their methods and the more difficult it becomes to correct a wrong technique or approach. He felt that far too many coaches had been coming from abroad only to stay for a short time, during which period they would concentrate on adults. He advocated the setting-up of training camps for coaches who would then train further coaches until eventually every school and college would have a qualified person in place. When he became Chairman of the Public Services Commission of the Saurashtra State in 1954 and then a member of the All-India Council of Sports, he was able to influence The Union Ministry of Education to hold a cricket camp at Rajkot, where he had been educated. Duleep was in charge with the mission of training these coaches. After the merger of the Union of Saurashtra with the state of Bombay, Duleep joined as a member of the Bombay State Public Services Commission of which he was a member from 1956 to 1958 and was appointed Chairman on June 3, 1958. He led a month's camp at Khadakvasla for members of the military and also led a further camp at Delhi which had been organised by the Board of Control. He held very strong views on all aspects of how to play the game and these would form the basis of his discussions with the embryo coaches. Such points as how to behave, how to approach a game, how to dress and how to be a member of a team were just as important as his considered views on technical areas as stance, grip of the bat, back-lift, various strokes and advice for bowlers and fielders. He was tireless in his speech and writings on expressing these viewpoints. His passionate advocacy of these strongly-held beliefs must have been instrumental in gaining the support of the Board of Control and was further evidence of just how influential and persuasive he had become!

Duleep's views on the role of a coach went far beyond the mere supervising of net practice and hitting up a few catches which had been his experience with so many that he had seen. A proper coach would make his pupil "cricket-literate" with the responsibility of educating his pupil in the traditions of cricket and the code of conduct expected from those playing this "greatest of games". He had thought carefully about the way in which a coach should be trained, having analysed the necessary requirements. The ideal coach which he was aiming to produce would obviously be one who would be able to spot quickly and then correct faults of technique, but just as importantly he would be able to make his charges realise that cricket was a team game, a game of discipline and commitment. All aspects of the game would be discussed, such as captaincy, selection, field placings and the thinking behind bowling changes. He should not discourage his pupils from playing certain shots which he deemed faulty, but rather should he try to make the boy play this stroke correctly if it were not "unscientific". It was essential that the coach had a personality and competence which made his pupils respect him and even regard him as a friend.

Perhaps his most strongly-held belief in the area of coaching was that resources be concentrated on the younger members of the community rather than on the top levels. He felt that there was far too much attention given to Test tours, home and abroad, the building of large stadia and to "those cricketers whose technique has already been hardened in the wrong mould". He thought it far more beneficial to Indian cricket to have fifty playing fields costing 100,000 rupees each than have one impressive stadium costing fifty times that amount. The foundation of the game lay in the schools where it should be encouraged. A youngster could benefit greatly from a good coach and one could not over-estimate the value of sport in the development of a person's character. A strong believer in *mens sana in corpore sano,* he was of the opinion that there was far too much emphasis on examinations in schools at the expense of a more-balanced curriculum and in this respect, as in many others, one can appreciate how far-sighted he was. In our country today so many summer extra-curricular activities have been seriously curtailed by the non-stop examinations endured by staff and pupils alike.

When on June 7, 1947, Duleep officially opened the school built by The Maharajah of Porbandar, his interest in coaching and encouraging the young was again clearly to be seen. As a result of his efforts in these areas, the school was named "The Duleep School of Cricket" in his honour and he took the opportunity to emphasise his ideals. To Duleep's delight the school had four differing wickets which would give youngsters the chance to bat and bowl on various surfaces, each one becoming more difficult. For one who was such a great fielder himself, he always emphasised the importance of this part of the game which made him delighted to see an up-to-date slip-catching device for practice. He was critical of the authorities yet again for being responsible for causing an atmosphere in which the winning of gold cups and trophies was considered more important than spending time and money on India's future players. For the first time it could be seen that an effort was being made to produce cricketers with a sound technique. Again he stressed the need for appointing expert coaches who followed guidelines.

Amongst his many schemes to promote cricket in particular and sport in general for the benefit of youngsters was what he called his Five-Year Plan. With regard to this, his belief in the benefits of sport for the correct development of a teenager's character could not be more obvious. As well as again emphasising his belief in "catching them young" and acquiring suitable coaches, he placed great stress on the character-building aspects of games. With the right leadership from the outset, sport was capable of developing character, leadership, discipline, personality and temperament. It was an aid to reducing poor behaviour in schools and should be looked upon as an essential part of education. Physical fitness was an obvious benefit, but so, too, was the development of team spirit. The opportunity to organise should not be overlooked in a summary of the benefits. To do all this there had to be far more commitment to the building of sports fields with the full co-operation of the Union Ministry of Education. If all his ideas were to be put in place, with the full co-operation of governmental and educational bodies, Duleep felt that in five years' time Indian sport would begin to see the benefits - a stumbling block to overcome would be the "professional office-bearers", the getting rid of whom was " a pressing problem".

In later years, as we have seen, he was in a position to implement many of his schemes. Although fully occupied in so many areas, he still found time to attend to his mission of holding coaching classes and camps to produce coaches. Right up to his death in 1959 he was working on schemes for the improvement of cricket in India; his aim was simply to raise Indian cricket to the highest possible standards. Just before he died he formulated a scheme for the setting up of an All-India Sports Institute which was subsequently accepted by the Indian Government. He accepted the position of honorary Director of the Institute as he felt that it was his responsibility to steer it in the right direction.

11.

A FULL LIFE

Duleepsinhji as journalist and diplomat

WE HAVE SEEN HOW Duleep's time on his return to India was largely occupied with helping his brother in affairs of state as he became the Jam Saheb of Nawanagar on Ranji's death, and in various spells as a Test selector. Towards the end of his life he became very heavily involved in various official positions and in the development of adolescents' opportunities to play sport and be correctly taught, as has been noted. That, however, is not the end of the story as in the period between being a selector and taking on the roles of Chairman of the Saurashtra, then Bombay Public Services Commission, and the All-India Council of Sports, he worked as a respected cricket journalist before becoming the Indian High Commissioner to Australia and New Zealand.

Prior to the Indian tour of England in 1946, the first official Test tour after World War II, he wrote an article in April in *The Free Press Journal* giving advice and encouragement to the players about to set off. He felt that English cricket would be in an unhealthy state because of the war and if the fielders supported the bowlers, with the batsmen scoring quickly, many county matches could be won. Perhaps mindful of the dissension and ill-discipline which had been such a feature of India's previous tour to England in 1936, emphasis was laid on team spirit and mutual respect. The players were "not to take their quarrels on the field. All arguments and squabbles must be left behind."

He proceeded to write regularly throughout the tour articles from India under the title *At This Distance* in which, using his experience of English conditions, he gave advice on the pitches likely to be encountered in the earlier games at Worcester, the Oval and Fenner's with reference to varied weather conditions. His familiarity with English pitches was clearly seen when after the first day's play at a rain-stricken Leicester, he analysed the effect that the elements would have had with regard to the use of covers. The "sweating" of the pitch, causing an irregular surface, was one of the hazards which batsmen had to overcome, not too easy for those brought up in India. The positive side of this, however, was that the changing surface conditions in England made playing there so interesting and would help to make more complete players. Indian cricketers would also benefit from the amount of cricket played on a tour in England, probably as much in one season as in five or six in India. The ever-changing weather conditions in England could make the game one of great excitement, but at the end of the tour he did not feel that enough of India's cricketers had coped well enough. Unfortunately,

it was evident that "Our weakness is that we are
fair-weather cricketers." He was critical, too, of
too many changes in the batting order, which he
likened to expecting soccer players to alternate
between being forwards and defenders. In this
opinion Duleep was supported by Wally
Hammond, England's captain in the series, who
said later that Pataudi was too ready to alter his
batting order, even after the order had been
written down; batsmen do not like this
uncertainty. It is not quite obvious what he was
referring to, but he was critical of captains who
concentrated on creating records rather than
allowing events to bring these about in the normal
course of play. It has been suggested, however,
that after his rival for the captaincy, Vijay
Merchant, had scored 242* against Lancashire,
Pataudi allowed Vijay Hazare a week later to bat
on unnecessarily against Yorkshire to score 244*
and thus beat him. Finally, he was also no
believer in allowing averages to become too
important as the quality of the opposition, the
state of the game and the conditions had to be
taken into account.

These same qualities of advice and being
unafraid to be critical were also in evidence
when he covered the Indian tour of Australia in
1947/48. Before the team set out, he wrote
articles in *The Times of India* calling on his
experiences as a player there some seventeen
years earlier as well as drawing lessons from the
England tour of 1946/47. He based his
authority on the fact that only two Indian
cricketers had played there before, himself and

the Nawab of Pataudi, and gave his opinions on what to expect, such as great hospitality, which is "hearty and open-handed," and the fact that cricket was a national obsession. The size of the grounds, the candour of Australian crowds and the need to be careful in statements to their Press, when only the captain and the manager should make statements, and then only when necessary, were topics covered. He warned his compatriots that Australia played to win, an attitude which India must copy with emphasis being given to studying the strengths and weaknesses of their opponents.

He was critical of many Indian players who had faulty strokes, which they would have to learn to correct before going there, and the bowlers would have to learn quickly how to adapt to Australian conditions. He was a little pessimistic in this respect as he felt that as few as two or three players had benefited from the tour of England. The Indian Board of Control ought to have sent out a scout to Australia in the previous season to learn about such matters as the Australian team, the pitches and the type of players India would need. He was very unhappy about the side which had been selected as it contained too many batsmen and not enough bowlers. One had to remember that a bowler's task was much harder than that of a batsman. Then, with some advice which is just as pertinent in 2005, he warned the Indian players from feeling that the Australians were much superior. If you were to start the tour with this feeling of inferiority, you have as good as already lost before leaving home.

After these preliminary articles he went out to see the Indians in Australia as a correspondent for Reuters. His efforts to try to give some advice to the captain, Lala Amarnath, were not too well received as Amarnath felt that he was interfering and became rather brusque in his attitude towards him. Some of the points Duleep made in his summary of the tour are very critical of the leadership and one wonders whether the points he raised are ones that he brought up with the captain and which were rejected. As had been the case during the 1946 tour of England, he could not come to terms with the continuous changing of the batting order which he felt was disruptive to the best players in the side. The bowlers did not take advantage of the "sticky" wickets they encountered, as instead of bowling a full length on the wicket, they tended to bowl too short and off the wicket which presumably the management should have corrected. The captain was loathe to consult his bowlers as regards field-placing, which made them "lose confidence and heart". Moreover, the fielding was below standard and practice in this vital area was neglected; even if there were some attempts to improve this aspect of the game, the net practices were poorly organised. The futility of good batsmen being bowled to by non-bowlers in the net was also strongly criticised, the natural talent of the Indian side was not brought out, and, all in all, the Indian side was not up to the Australian standards in any area and "lacked knowledge of the finer points". The lack of fast bowling and recognised opening batsmen had been a grievous handicap. It is hardly any wonder, is it, that Amarnath did not welcome his company?

What is strange here, perhaps, is that Wally Hammond in his book *Cricket My World* is full of praise for the efforts of Amarnath on this tour. He described his handling of the Indian team as masterly, especially as the material he had i.e. the players, was "patchy" and the weather against him was wretched. After dealing with the cruel luck in some of the Tests, Hammond sums up Amarnath's efforts as being such as to prove that to be captain of one's country and to lead it with gallantry and skill, it is not necessary to be of royal lineage.

In retrospect one may feel that Duleep was being a little harsh in seemingly placing all the Indians in the categories of failures. Vijay Hazare's century in each innings in the Adelaide Test, Vinoo Mankad's centuries in both Melbourne Tests in addition to some sterling bowling performances, merit more credit than is given in a more or less blanket condemnation of the team, although to be fair to him he did give Hazare a beautiful gold cigarette case in honour of his achievement. What is of interest is the performance with the bat of the captain himself. In matches outside the Tests he made such scores as 228*, 172*, 171, 144, 135 and 94* which gave him an average of over 100, yet in the Tests themselves he made a mere 140 runs in the same number of completed innings. This recalls similar experiences with Denis Compton in Australia 1950/51 and Peter May in South Africa 1956/57.

Duleep had twice been to Australia, as a cricketer in 1929, when he had made a great impression, and in the 1947/48 season as a journalist covering the Indian tour when he had again impressed most people, except perhaps Amarnath! He had found both these visits immensely enjoyable as he loved the country and its people.

In 1950 came a third visit of far more importance than the previous two, as he was appointed High Commissioner for the newly independent India to Australia and New Zealand. As one would expect, he threw himself into the job whole-heartedly, gaining himself great respect. At the end of his tenure some three and a half years later in 1953, he gave some glimpses of a diplomat's life. It was a wonderful experience with never a dull moment. He had heard the saying that a diplomat was a person who was sent out to lie for his country, but this he would like to refute! A diplomat had to be able to present his government's views courteously, yet forcefully enough to be taken account of. It was a rather awesome experience to be representing the views of some 300 million people. In his position he had to encourage tourism to his country and promote its culture. In a typical day, after dealing with the copious mail, he would receive many visitors and be dealing with a variety of topics concerned with his country. It was also necessary to find time to deal with the press and all these visitors had to be listened to and answered. Sometimes silly questions would test all the "diplomatic" skills he had, but a smile could be very effective. Duleep looked upon Australia as being the "bridge between European and Asiatic civilisations", a very important factor in his approach to the job.

Although it was soon evident that Duleep did not look upon his position as a sinecure, one that had been obtained through his eminence as a cricketer, it was of great help to him, certainly in the initial stages, that the Australian Prime Minister was the cricket-loving Robert Menzies. The Indian Prime Minister, Pandit Nehru, had written to Mr. Menzies to the effect that because of his personal qualities and his varied experiences, he had great confidence in Duleep. He knew that "Shri Duleepsinhji will prove eminently fitted for the work entrusted to him." Duleep recalled that whenever he visited Mr. Menzies on official business, the first half-hour or so would be occupied with talk about cricket. That his beloved uncle was never far from his mind was evident in his sitting room in Canberra where several cigar cases which had belonged to Ranji were prominently displayed, as well as a silver cigarette case with an inscription teasing Duleep for being out to an indiscriminate stroke in an important game - shades of Lord's 1930!

His diplomatic skills were in evidence during the West Indies tour of Australia in 1951/52. The West Indies were enjoying a particularly good session in a Test when another guest at lunch made the comment within everybody's hearing: "Your Excellency, your boys have done well this morning." Duleep would no doubt have given his customary warm smile and thanked him for his sentiments. A similar case of mistaken identity had occurred in his playing days when the Prince of Wales, eager to appear cognizant with the players' histories, asked questions about Duleep's

Oxford days whilst crediting Ian Peebles with a Cambridge education. It is said that neither man was amused, but each of them passed off the incident as diplomatically as possible!

RS Whitington, who had previously met him as a member of the Australian Services side in India just after the war in 1945, saw him as a man "who treats people in the way they would wish to be treated, seems more interested in their way of life than in his own. A very interesting companion with very liberal views on most subjects."

There is a very interesting section in a book called *Green is the Grass* describing an interview with him during his time in Australia. The book is written by an extraordinarily precocious thirteen-year-old boy called Dom Moraes, who was visiting the country on a round-the-world trip with his father Frank, editor of *The Times of India*. He writes as follows: "Kumar Shri Duleepsinhji - his humorous, quizzical brown eyes twinkling over the aquiline nose and those full pursed lips; his long, slim hands moving quickly as he illustrated his point, the Indian High Commissioner in Australia smiled at me from his arm chair." Was this "quiet man with the profile of a rather cherubic Grecian god, clad in a neat grey suit" the same one who had destroyed Australia's bowlers at Lord's in 1930 in scintillating style? Moraes then goes on to describe how Duleep "radiates a quiet charm, a simplicity and old-world nobility not given to many in this Atomic Age. His mild, calm spirit is reflected in his shy, but endearing demeanour, and his slightly husky voice." He next proceeded to give the youngster a batting tutorial emphasising the need to keep the head over the ball; to keep a straight bat; to get the left leg out for forward strokes and to be relaxed for cutting. Even eighteen years after his death Ranji's presence is still strong as he tells the boy that his uncle told him to have six strokes for every ball and that a straight bat was the "foundation stone for a century". His awe and veneration for Ranji was to be seen in his collection of cigarette and cigar cases from his uncle's heirlooms. He wrote that Duleep and his charming princess have made a great impression on the Australian public.

Perhaps it is not surprising to learn that this boy later wrote poetry which was highly commended by WH Auden and published by Stephen Spender. In 1956 he went to Jesus College, Cambridge, to read English.

During this West Indies tour Duleep was persuaded to try his hand at umpiring in the game at Canberra between the Prime Minister's XI and the tourists. His fellow umpire was the ex-Australian fast-bowler Ernie McCormick, the man who had started his country's 1938 tour of England at Worcester with thirty-five no-balls, including seventeen in the first two overs. Before the match it had been arranged by Robert Menzies with the umpires that no batsman should be given out before he had scored, as many of his side had not played for some time There were to be no LBW or caught behind decisions in the early stages of a batsman's innings and a no-ball was to be called immediately if a player were blatantly out. The first ball of the match from John Trim was edged to second slip by ex-Test opener Jack Fingleton, to be caught comfortably by Everton Weekes. Obviously the West Indians were not in on the plan and appealed. As described by onlooker Don Seith, McCormick, "overcome by the suddenness of it all, forgot the instructions Menzies had given him, and raising his arm horizontally to signal No-Ball, raised it vertically to signal Out." Fingleton was livid, but there was nothing he could do - he had to go! If Duleep had been at the bowler's end, would he have remembered his instructions and, using his diplomatic skills, have prolonged the innings of the prominent author/journalist? During the game both umpires were relieved by Arthur Mailey, the former Australian spin bowler turned cartoonist, and Vin Griffiths, reputed to be the best umpire in the capital.

12.

FRAGILE BEAUTY

Duleepsinhji and
Archie Jackson compared

IT IS REMARKABLE and an accident of history how two such batsmen as Duleep and Jackson, with a similar style of enchanting batsmanship yet tragically similar health problems, appeared at the same time in the cricket world in the 1920's. Each one was hailed as his country's champion, yet each one was in fact from overseas.

As we have seen, Duleep was born in India in 1905, but to all intents and purposes was brought up in England for which country he appeared in Test matches. Archie Jackson was born in Scotland, but at the age of three his family emigrated to Australia for which country he played Test cricket.

Although there was this similarity in each of them being born outside the country in which they achieved their fame, their backgrounds were strikingly different. Duleep came from a very privileged background of rulers and princes, and attended a prestigious public school before going on to Cambridge University at the age of 19 after having had a year "out". Jackson's father worked in a dockyard in Sydney after an earlier career managing a brickworks and Archie left school at 15 with a brilliant sporting record behind him. Duleep was very strongly subsidised financially by Uncle Ranji, whereas Jackson earned his living after leaving school by working first of all in a warehouse and then in a sports shop owned by that superb batsman Alan Kippax. He had, however, received some financial assistance from Arthur Mailey, ex-Australian spin "wizard", and Dr HV Evatt who later became a famous politician.

From an early age it was obvious that both of them were going to be outstanding cricketers, Duleep exciting attention at Cheltenham College and Jackson at Balmain Cricket Club after having gained state representative schoolboy honours. Duleep made his first-class debut for MCC v Oxford University when he had just turned 19 before embarking on his Cambridge career in the following season, but Archie Jackson was a mere 17 when he was first selected to play for New South Wales at Brisbane in Queensland's first match in the Sheffield Shield competition.

The standard of their batting and the manner in which they scored their runs soon reached a much wider audience throughout the cricket-loving centres of their university/county or state, but what an amazing coincidence it was that both of them had a great contemporary, just slightly older, with whom they were flatteringly compared. In Duleep's case it was the mighty Walter Hammond with whom his name was often linked as being the two greatest of the young batting prospects; some critics even placed Duleep at No. 1 in this respect.

Archie Jackson's great contemporary was, of course, Don Bradman, also from New South Wales. In fact Jackson made his debut the season before Bradman even though over a year younger. The irony is that Bradman only made his debut as a replacement for Jackson as the latter had a painful boil on his knee. The game was New South Wales against South Australia at Adelaide and, with what was a foretaste of things to come, Bradman marked the occasion with the first of his centuries.

When we realise what Bradman was to become it is hard to imagine that many respected critics and players placed Jackson slightly above him at one stage. As the careers of all these four players can now be seen in their entirety, there is little doubt that Bradman is the greatest of all batsmen, whilst Hammond would be the choice of many to vie with Jack Hobbs as England's greatest-ever batsman. At the time, however, all this was not clear and although one cannot imagine Jackson, aesthetics apart, ever overtaking "The Don", there is perhaps more room for debate as to what Duleep's achievements may have been over the years given good health and a willingness to carry on playing. Certainly Duleep was cut off in his prime and in the years 1929-31 scored more runs than any of his contemporaries in cricket in England, ahead not only of Hammond, but also others such as Herbert Sutcliffe, Frank Woolley, Patsy Hendren and Jack Hobbs.

There was a remarkable parallel in the performances of these two great young batsmen in their debut in Ashes Tests. At Adelaide in the

1928/29 series Jackson made his debut in the fourth Test of a series dominated by England, particularly by the batting of Hammond who in this match scored 119* and 177. Jackson opened the innings with Bill Woodfull but soon lost him, "Stork" Hendry and his New South Wales colleague Alan Kippax, to leave the score at 19 for 3 with the innings seemingly in tatters. The young Bradman in only his third Test batting at number 6 - he had been at 7 in his first Test! - gave great assistance to Archie with 40. Jackson finished with 164, an innings that made him a national hero and, so we are told, brought tears to the eyes of even hardened men. It was an innings played in searing heat with an amazing performance from England's slow left-arm bowler Jack "Farmer" White who bowled 60 overs for 5-130 to be followed in the second innings with 64.5 overs to finish with 8-126. In a very closely contested game with Jackson scoring 36 in the second innings, England just managed to win by 12 runs.

The Ashes debut of Duleep has been dealt with at length in a previous chapter, but as a quick reminder he scored 173 in 1930 at Lord's to receive similar accolades to those granted to Jackson at Adelaide. On both occasions it was not so much a matter of the size of the innings, important as this was, as the manner of them as far as beauty of stroke-play was concerned, the temperament shown on the big occasion and the rescuing of the innings, after a moderate start in England's case and a disastrous one by Australia.

Both these young men are renowned for the elegance of their batting and the delight given to all who saw them. Australians were always looking for a new Victor Trumper, just as later there was always excitement as a new Bradman could emerge. Jackson's style of batting appeared to be very close to that of Trumper with his classical method, easy grace of style and dazzling array of shots all round the wicket with perhaps the late-cut, that favourite of the connoisseur, the most eye-catching. In his early days there were certain reservations about his fallibility outside the off-stump, but he worked hard to overcome this defect. He came to England with the 1930 Australian side but generally struggled, with health problems being a significant factor. He did, however, play one innings of great significance in the final Test at the Oval on the fourth day. After a rather uncomfortable session on the previous day, he and Bradman resumed their partnership on a very lively wicket with Larwood in particular being very difficult to cope with. Jackson was hit several times on the body but never flinched, whereas Bradman seemed distinctly ill at ease in one period. This is said to have given rise to the planning of the "Bodyline" campaign as it was the only sign of weakness that he seemed to have, even though he finished the innings with 232! Jackson finished with 73, an innings which caused "Plum" Warner to comment: " .....we saw something of the style and grace which have caused him to be compared, in some measure, with Trumper by Australian critics."

All the adjectives used about the glory of Jackson's stroke-play are equally applicable to Duleep. Under Aubrey Faulkner's excellent tutelage he also worked hard to overcome a weakness outside the off-stump and in addition developed his off-side play. The late-cut was also a particular glory of Duleep's style. He had that wonderful suppleness of wrist and exquisite timing seen in so many great players from the Indian sub-continent, whereby they appear to charm the ball to the boundary with minimum effort. In modern times one thinks of such as Azharuddin and Dravid who possess this great gift. Just as Jackson had Trumper as a model with whom he was continually compared, so too did Duleep have an example to follow. It was inevitable that the skills of his uncle, the great Ranjitsinhji, would be used as a benchmark. Ranji, the greatest batsman in England at the turn of the nineteenth century, a man who never "played a Christian stroke in his life", was the very epitome of Oriental grace and style. He is forever associated with "inventing" the leg-glance, a stroke which, when well-executed, brings gasps of admiration from the cognoscenti.

So much for the comparisons of the batting genius of these great players; we now have to come to the tragedy of the parallels in their early retirement from the game. As we have seen, Duleep had to retire at the age of 27 when he should have been at the height of his powers, but at least he did live long enough to play several roles in Indian life before dying at the very early age of 54.

Archie Jackson also suffered from pulmonary tuberculosis which first manifested itself as early as the 1929/30 season. He was not in good health during the 1930 tour of England where he was not helped by the damp and cold weather of much of the summer.

He was not even well enough to meet the King and Queen at Sandringham, normally a highlight of any touring cricketer's visit.

The situation became worse on his return to Australia and, just as happened with Duleep, he started to cough up blood and suffer from exhaustion. Rather than the sanatoria of Switzerland, as in Duleep's case, Archie attended one in the Blue Mountains in his home state of New South Wales. He then went on to live in Queensland where he thought that the warmer weather would be beneficial to him. In the season of 1932/33 he started to play Grade cricket in Brisbane for Northern Suburbs, or Norths, as they are known locally. In spite of his obvious problems with breathing and stamina he proceeded to score an enormous number of runs before large appreciative crowds. He had hoped to start playing for Queensland and was even very optimistic about returning to the Australian side and touring England in 1934.

However, by February of 1933 he had become very ill and was admitted into hospital after collapsing on the field. The fourth Test with England was played at the Brisbane ground of Woolloongabba near to the hospital where Jackson lay suffering. He died at the age of 23 on January 16, the very day that England won back the Ashes. With a supreme touch of irony, the winning hit for six was made by Eddie Paynter who had come into the touring party as a replacement for the sick Duleepsinhji. In the first innings Paynter had become part of cricket's folklore when, after having been admitted to hospital with tonsillitis, he "rose from his sick bed" on the orders of Jardine and scored 83 to avert a crisis.

These two wonderful cricketers, Duleep and Jackson, who had so much to offer the world of cricket, were cut off in their prime with only twenty Tests between them. How might the romantic side of cricket's history been changed had they been allowed full career spans!

13.

RANJITSINHJI AND DULEEPSINHJI

THE NAME OF Ranjitsinhji, or Ranji, has figured very prominently so far in the text, so it may be appropriate at this stage to say something about his cricket career and status in the game before going on to discuss his relationship with his nephew.

In what many commentators and critics term the Golden Age of cricket, Ranji was the most glittering star of all. After an unexceptional career at Cambridge University where he won his Blue in 1893, he went on to play for Sussex where he developed quickly into becoming the finest batsman of his generation in an age of great players. He was a prolific run-scorer and in 1899 he became the first batsman in the game's history to score 3,000 runs in a season. He repeated the feat the following season with an average of 87.57, scored over 2,000 runs on another three occasions and over 1,000 runs in a further six seasons. He scored 72 centuries, including 14 doubles, with a highest score of 285* v Somerset at Taunton, which remained the highest score for Sussex until his nephew scored 333 at Hove v Northampton in 1930. He scored his runs at the very impressive average of 56.37 and held 233 catches, mainly in the slips.

In Test cricket he made his debut at Old Trafford in 1896 v Australia when he made a most auspicious start with 62 and 154*, including a century before lunch, the first instance in Test cricket of this feat. The whole cricketing nation knew that he should have been chosen for the first Test at Lord's, but in the days when Test sides were chosen by the ground authority of the centre where the Test was to be held, MCC would not select him because of his Indian nationality; Lord Harris declared him to be "a bird of passage". Fortunately, the Old Trafford authorities had no such inhibitions. In his first Test in Australia he scored 175 at Sydney which was to remain his highest score in his fifteen Tests for England with just under 1,000 runs at an average of 44.95. One of his most famous feats was against Yorkshire when he scored a century in each innings on the same day at Hove in 1896. Punch christened him "Run-get-Sinhji" and one Cockney spectator, overcome with admiration, called upon "Ramsgate Jimmy" as he effortlessly glided yet another boundary to the fence.

However, impressive as they are, these are cold figures which do not tell us enough about his sheer genius and his impact on the game. He revolutionised the art of batting in England with his magical stroke-play and quickness of eye. He had that wristiness in his shots which we now so associate with Indian cricketers and perfected, perhaps invented, the leg-glance with which his name has become so inextricably bound. In an age of forward attacking play with back-play being merely for defence, he became a master of attacking shots off the back foot. He displayed shots never before seen in his adopted country, all made with such ease and grace.

He was said to "charm" the ball to the boundary and after having done this on several occasions to the Yorkshire bowler Tom Emmett, the latter is alleged to have declared that "Ranji has never played a Christian stroke in his life!" An umpire of his period said that he was a greater batsman than the great WG Grace himself because he had more strokes. His great companion, the eminent Sussex cricketer CB Fry, said of him that " he moved as if he had no bones: one would not be surprised to see brown curves burning in the grass where one of his cuts had travelled, or blue flame shimmering round his bat as he made one of his leg strokes." His county captain said, "All other batsmen are labourers in comparison." The *Daily News* journalist AG Gardiner wrote of him so vividly: "There is little display in his methods - an Oriental calm with an Occidental swiftness, the stillness of the panther with the suddenness of its spring. Nothing happens except that one sudden flash, perfectly timed, indisputable. If the supreme art is to achieve the maximum result with the minimum expenditure of effort, then Ranji is in a class by himself."

It may now have become a cliché, but the finest sight on a cricket field in late-Victorian England must have been this exquisite stroke-player batting in fluttering shirtsleeves, buttoned at the wrist, gliding the ball effortlessly to the boundary at Hove. "The shirt, always of silk, always fully large, was his most distinctive feature. It bellied and flapped round his body like a sail at every movement of the breeze. And there he stood at the wicket the very embodiment of grace and elegance, almost careless and lazy in attitude, so perfect and relaxed was the whole poise of the slight delicate figure." The glamour of his background from an Indian princely family when that distant land and vital part of the British Empire was in itself a source of fascination merely added to his charisma.

The Illustrated London News of June 17 1893 wrote a feature on him when he was aged only 20 which showed how he had captured the imagination of the public. The great pervading atmosphere of Empire and its link with cricket in the sub-continent is clearly noticeable:

An Indian Prince on the cricket-field earning the applause of the most critical crowds by his brilliant batting is a spectacle sufficiently novel to awaken the sympathy of all who have a spark of interest in either the vast Empire from which the player comes or in the great national game which is so characteristic of England. Kumar Shri Ranjitsinhji, whose excellent achievements in the Cambridge University Eleven have led to his obtaining the coveted honour of a place in the annual inter-University match, is a Rajput Prince of Jadeja descent and a relative of Jamnagar. After study at Rajkumar College, in Rajkot, he came to England in 1888, and two years later he entered Trinity College, Cambridge. In 1891 he had, by his cricketing

161

prowess, won his college colours, and at the end of the season his average was fifty-four runs. In addition, he is an excellent player at tennis and racquets and a good shot. Mr. Ranjitsinhji has had this season remarkable success with the bat, scoring 58 and 37 (not out) in the match against the Australians on June 10. Many years ago the Prince of Wales occasionally took part in a game of cricket at the Oval, while the sons of Prince Christian have constantly gained honours in the game. It is particularly appropriate that in these days when the "crimson thread of kinship" is, happily, a popular idea, an Indian prince should play for an ancient English University in the year when the Imperial Institute was opened.

He seemed unique until along came his nephew Duleepsinhji. He, too, played in a manner which set him apart from his contemporaries. His name is still revered by those in Sussex old enough to remember him or those who had fathers who hero-worshipped him. Ranji, having no children of his own, dedicated much of his time and money to the four sons of his younger brother of whom the youngest was Duleep. As soon as it was evident that his was a burgeoning talent, Ranji devoted more and more time encouraging him, spending hours coaching him, thus laying the foundations of his technique.

Ranji was then instrumental in gaining a place for his nephew, first of all at his prep school in England of St Faith's and then at Cheltenham

College. Ranji paid his fees and supported him in general financially. As Duleep's name started to be known by a wider audience, Ranji's influence became more and more discernible and inevitably comparisons were beginning to be made, more so after his powers of persuasion had found a place for him at Clare College, Cambridge. The youngster's introduction into first-class cricket caused tremendous interest. There were those, of course, who would never admit that Duleep could be anything like as good as his uncle. Having such a notable relative in one's sport is both an advantage and a handicap. In more modern times one thinks of what a mixed blessing it has been for those such as Richard Hutton and the Cowdrey brothers when they were continually compared with their illustrious fathers, Len and Colin. Richard's standard answer to those who said he was not as good as his father was that not too many were! That delightful writer AA Thompson said, "Ranji began his career under the handicap of an English lack of imagination which could not conceive the notion of an Indian as a cricketer. Ranji's brilliant nephew, KS Duleepsinhji, suffered a handicap even more difficult to surmount for he had to work out his own salvation under the shadow of his almost impossibly brilliant uncle."

Ranji's attitude to his nephew was rather ambivalent as although basically very proud of him, he could be rather hurtful in his sarcasm. For instance, when towards the end of the 1926 season at Cambridge, Duleep was having a poor run, Ranji sent him a telegram to suggest he gave up cricket to go and play tennis with Betty Nuttall. Ranji no doubt thought this to be funny, but Duleep didn't. There was reproof at Lord's in 1930 when after scoring a glorious century he was caught in the deep by Bradman and heard the verdict that "the boy was always careless". There were also the occasions when Duleep would be taunted by Ranji telling him that the other Indian prince in English cricket, namely the Nawab of Pataudi, was a better player, which was just not true. The saddest instance of all was, of course, in 1932 when Duleep was so ill and trying to struggle on to lead his county to the County Championship and his uncle, himself recovering from treatment at Aix-les-Bains in France, sent him a very cruel telegram: "I did not know I had a member in my family who would let his side and his county down at a critical time." Duleep felt compelled to play and in so doing suffered irreparable damage to his lungs. Ranji, who did not appreciate the extent of the damage to his nephew at the time, was mortified.

There was an early occasion, however, when he was most encouraging to his nephew when the latter was expecting to be criticised after being dismissed first ball during a disappointing sequence of scores. He was summoned to Ranji's home in Staines thinking he may even be advised to give up the game. However, his uncle told him that he had been thinking a lot about his cricket. He told him that after his serious illness in 1927, ninety-nine out of a hundred cricketers would never have attempted to play again. He went on: "I advise you to continue, and you will find your old form. You will play for England one day..." He was also very generous in his praise of him when he scored his celebrated 115 and 246 at Hastings in 1929. One who knew both of them felt that even the Jam Saheb would have been delighted with his nephew's glorious cricket. Ranji did in fact send him a telegram offering his warmest congratulations, adding the comment: "This is how you should treat modern bowling."

Until the very end of his life Ranji was most generous in financial matters, providing him with day-to-day expenses and paying for treatment in health centres abroad. As Duleep's career progressed so successfully, Ranji became more and more the proud uncle. He took exception though to reports that he gave a reward to his nephew for every run over a century. "That is unfair to a family that has done all that lies in its power to sustain the best traditions of British sportsmanship," he said angrily.

Duleep's attitude to his uncle was one of almost complete awe and reverence. Sir Home Gordon, who knew both of them well, felt that in Ranji's presence Duleep showed something of an inferiority complex, always appearing to feel that he was in the company of his state ruler rather than that of his uncle. So many of his remarks were prefaced with "Uncle says...." or "Uncle thinks..." Ranji was the beginning and the end of cricket knowledge as far as Duleep was concerned. When "uncle" spoke all others had to remain silent. He could never believe that he approached the standards of batsmanship of his uncle. On one occasion after he had scored four centuries in quick succession, an outstanding retired Test player congratulated him in the dressing room at Hove with the words that he had never enjoyed such brilliant batsmanship for years and that he was an even finer bat than his uncle. This was too much for Duleep who replied that he could not agree with the statement and that he would never be the player that his uncle was as he was truly a great batsman. With his uncle he sometimes gave the feeling that he was on edge and not comfortable, a feeling that was not helped by Ranji implying at times that perhaps Duleep was over-rated. Learie Constantine noted how over-awed Duleep was when playing in front of his uncle with this continual comparison. Ranji on the surface rarely seemed satisfied and would be critical if Duleep made a high score but then got out. Duleep would have given anything for his uncle to have shown total appreciation. The influence which Ranji had over his nephew can clearly be seen in the club minutes of April 29, 1929, when "The Secretary was instructed to send a cable in reply to the one received from the <u>Jam Sahib of Nawanagar</u>, thanking him for allowing <u>K.S.Duleepsinhji</u> to play for Sussex this season." Although there is no doubt that financial considerations were very important for Duleep in his decision to play, the really crucial factor would have been Ranji's control over Duleep's life.

He did give him some kind words, however, at the beginning of his career after a school match at Lord's when he told him that he had a God-given talent. "If you want to play cricket, I will give you every help you need, but you will have to remember that when you are playing, you are not playing for yourself but for your country. Thousands of English people will be watching you play and millions reading the papers. To them you will be representing India. I don't want you to do anything you will be ashamed of later and do harm to your country. Remember that God has given you a gift which you can use for the benefit of India."

The death of Ranji caused Duleep great distress. When he heard the news, his temporary improvement in health was at an end and he suffered a further breakdown so serious that he had a lung removed and seemed to lose the will to live. He was weakened by further haemorrhaging causing his doctors almost to give up in despair. In this hour of crisis a cricket-loving doctor, Dr. Wilkinson, came on the scene. His methods of treating tuberculosis were considered unorthodox by the medical establishment but such was his confidence that his offer of help was accepted. Duleep was moved to Wentworth Dormy House in Surrey, still so ill that the haemorrhage left him in such weakness that for some time he was unable to move or speak. It was only after three months of treatment that Duleep was able to tell his brother at the bedside that he thought he had passed the crisis.

As with the sons of Len Hutton and Colin Cowdrey referred to previously, it is wrong to judge players repeatedly with reference to their distinguished relatives. It was inevitable that Ranji's name immediately came to mind whenever his nephew was discussed and comparisons would be made. This was very hard on Duleep as he was a great player in his own right, the best amateur batsman of his period and in the opinion of many leading critics and players a serious rival to those immortals, the professionals Walter Hammond and Herbert Sutcliffe, as the leading batsman of the late twenties and early thirties. No less a person than Jack Hobbs said to a journalist that he was just as good as his illustrious uncle and Sutcliffe commented on the atmosphere and expectation in the crowd when he emerged from the pavilion being similar to that afforded Ranji.

Wherever he played he thrilled spectators with the beauty and elegance of his stroke-play, the delicacy of his late-cutting, the power of his classical driving through mid-on and, increasingly, through the covers. He was venerated by followers everywhere, but particularly in Sussex, of course. I have received several letters and 'phone calls from elderly people in Sussex after the local press kindly printed a letter from me asking for any recollections or anecdotes about him. One lady, Mrs Margaret Diggle, wrote to tell me that she has a recollection of having him pointed out to her in his Cambridge days as she was passing by when he was fielding. As she only saw his back it is clear what an impact this experience had, and still has, on her! His 333 in 1930 was seen by Mr Dorrington of Hove, who has particularly vivid memories as he "skipped" lectures that day at Brighton Technical College and recalls that he "was a delight to watch. With every shot in the book plus some of his own invention all round the wicket." I wonder if his tutors forgave him when they found out the Local History he had just witnessed which he could bring into his studies!

Mr Brian Fletcher of Lewes recalls the famous match at Hastings in 1929 against Kent when Duleep scored 115 and 246. After the great "Tich" Freeman had been hit for five leg-side boundaries off the first five balls of an over, he somewhat belatedly placed more fielders in the area and bowled the last ball very wide of the leg-stump. Duleep's response, as Mr Fletcher after all these years so fondly and clearly remembers, was to step back and cut him for another four through the vacant slip area. Of such stuff are legends made! He describes him as the best stroke-maker he ever saw and in his opinion "there never has been and never will be any batsman like him".

Just to remind us of his wonderful skills as a slip-fielder, many recall the occasion at Hove when a very hard slash was made at a ball from Maurice Tate which was seemingly flashing to the boundary followed by all eyes including, it appeared, Duleep's. He had in fact caught it with his lightning reactions and slipped it under his sweater. No wonder that it was claimed he could catch a swallow in flight as is hinted at by 91-year-old Mr George Isted, also of Lewes. Mr Jack Offen, a 90-year-old from Hove, identifies the batsman as Patsy Hendren.

Going back to earlier times, there is a letter extant from a Mr Ted Beer, dressing room attendant at Hove, sympathising with his illness and hoping to see him leading the side in the following season - 1932. When it was finally obvious that there would be no immediate miracle cure, hence no return to the cricket field, as previously mentioned, the famous poet EV Lucas felt moved to write on December 6, 1933, " I now don't care much if next season never comes at all."

The tributes paid to him by his contemporaries are almost overwhelming in their praise of his superb batting, but they all acclaim equally his wonderfully modest manner, grace and gentlemanly bearing. These attributes, allied to his wizardry at the crease, explain why he was so universally popular wherever he went with fellow players, opponents, officials and spectators.

Since India became a fully-fledged Test nation, they have produced many great batsmen such as Vijay Merchant, Vijay Hazare, Sunil Gavaskar, Mohammad Azharuddin and Sachin Tendulkar, but I would not think that any of these master batsmen could eclipse the beauty and splendour of uncle and nephew, Ranji and Duleep, the first supreme oriental cricketers.

14.

INDIAN CRICKET POLITICS IN DULEEP'S ERA

THERE HAD BEEN touring sides to India from the United Kingdom in 1889/90 and 1892/93 when GF Vernon of Middlesex and Lord Hawke of Yorkshire had led amateur teams, and in 1902/03 when the Oxford University Authentics travelled there, but not until 1926/27 did an MCC party visit. The team was led by Arthur Gilligan, until recently the England captain, and in addition to the captain himself contained such eminent players as Maurice Tate, Bob Wyatt, Andrew Sandham and George Geary.

Gilligan was so impressed with the standard of cricket, especially after an All-India side replied to the MCC first-innings total of 362 with 437, that he went round the country wherever the team played trying to impress upon them the need for a proper central organisation. This was difficult in a country the size of India with strong religious and social differences, to say nothing of the intense rivalry between Bombay, Delhi and Calcutta. Gilligan was convinced that the impressive standards he had seen needed to be supported by a Board of Control.

During a match in Delhi a meeting was arranged with a group reflecting the supremacy of

171

Europeans in the Raj. The group consisted of Gilligan himself, Anthony de Mello, Maharaj Bhupendra Singh and Grant Govan, an English businessman who employed de Mello. The rivalry, particularly that between Calcutta and Bombay, was exacerbated by a JS Spenser who was secretary of the Bombay Gymkhana. His strong feelings, expressed in intemperate language against Calcutta, were revealed in a letter which he wrote to the Governor of Bombay. His attempts to preserve his anonymity by using a nom de plume fooled nobody and the whole exercise was in fact counter-productive.

The Board was set up in 1928 with Grant Govan as President and Anthony de Mello as Secretary. There was a background of political strife to its workings as in its early years there was a period of great instability marked by Gandhi's long march in protest against the British ban on salt. Nationalist Hindus refused to take part in any "official" cricket, whilst leading cricketers were asked not to take part in trials to select the 1932 team to England. The Quadrangular, India's major tournament, was suspended for four years and the proposed visit of an England team to India in 1930/31 was called off.

Perhaps the situation would have been improved if India's two most famous cricketers had taken part in the development of the game. Ranji steadfastly refused to take on an autocratic role similar to that of Lord Harris and Pelham Warner in English cricket. He felt that the time had come for him to make a complete break from cricket and devote himself entirely to affairs of state as the Jem Sahib; moreover, after all his years in English cricket with Cambridge University, Sussex and England, he felt that all his loyalties in this respect belonged to England.

Ranji was extremely diligent in his duties as the Jam Saheb and in his years in this position he made enormous developments in the city of Nawanagar. He oversaw the construction of buildings based on western architecture such as the Irwin Hospital, the Sajuba Girls' High School, the Dayaram Library, the Railway Station, the Nursery School, the Port Office, the Central Bank, the Vegetable Market and the Grain Market, as well as many palaces and statues. In addition, he was a leading member of the Indian Chamber of Princes, taking a leading part in shaping its policies.

He showed his loyalty to the crown and British Empire during the First World War by various cash donations, the giving of military equipment such as ambulances and other transport and by loaning his house in Middlesex for use as a hospital. He then volunteered his services to the British Army and was designated to join the staff of Field Marshal Sir John French as his ADC. He was rather upset at not being given enough to do of a responsible nature. As can be imagined, the appalling weather in France was not too congenial for those brought up in India and before long he was laid low by chilblains and asthma. Sick leave in England led to a dreadful accident when he lost his right eye to an errant shot during a shooting party in Yorkshire.

In spite of this he was desperate to return to the front, but was prevented from doing so by the marriage of his younger sister back in India, a marriage he tried in vain to have postponed until the end of the war. During this period back in India he began many of the improvements referred to above. He dearly wanted to return to France and was, in fact, offered a post on Douglas Haig's staff but his health and princely duties forbade this. He did, however, excel in organising events for Indians returning home from France. His state's contributions to the Allied cause was not bettered by any other in proportion to its size and resources. For his efforts to help the British cause he was awarded the GBE and promoted to lieutenant-colonel. With this as his background it is hardly surprising that Ranji insisted on his nephew's loyalty to England.

India were hoping that Duleep would become their first Test captain, but Ranji, whose influence was over-riding, forbade him to play for his native country. He said that he owed everything to England and this is where his cricketing future should lie. Duleep was very unhappy in this period and almost gave up the game.. He felt that he was being pulled in all directions by his uncle, India and England. His refusal to captain or even play for India was misinterpreted by many people as an attempt to carry on playing for England as at that time India were a much weaker side He was also blamed for not being more active in the administration of cricket in the country after his retirement there, allegations which have been emphatically disproved in earlier chapters. The power-politics which were so pervasive in Indian cricket, as witnessed by their Board of Control's conduct during this period, were responsible for keeping Duleep out of the high position he merited for some years.

The struggle left him a bitter man, causing him later to vent his feelings on Govan and de Mello in language unworthy of him as he saw himself as a pawn in a game where people were out for personal glory. He refused even to captain the Hindus in the Quadrangular competition. The resulting impasse caused the Indian Board of Control to consider following the West Indies policy of making a white man captain. The most popular choice to approach was Douglas Jardine who was born in India and came from a family with a long history of service there. How would cricket history have changed if this plan had come to fruition?

That Duleep was well to the forefront of the Cricket Board of India's thinking is clearly seen in a letter sent to him on December 9 1929 from Bombay whilst he was in Australia on the MCC tour to Australia and New Zealand. The letter is signed by the President, Grant Govan, and says as follows:

KS Duleepsinhji Esq.,
C/o The MCC touring Team,
New Zealand

Dear Sir,

As you are probably aware the MCC are expected to tour India in the cold weather of

1930, arriving about the 11th October and sailing from Colombo about the 6th .March 1931. We are making a preliminary forecast of the cricketing talent which will be available in the country and in this connection I am writing to enquire whether you expect to be in India during this period.

You are also doubtless aware that India are arranging to send a Team to tour England in the summer of 1932.

The fixture list will consist of a few preliminary practice games and 25 Matches as follows:

17 first class Counties
1 Minor combined Counties
1 Cambridge University
1 Oxford University
1 MCC
2 Festival Matches
1 Wales
1 Test Match

We are asking England for one Test Match, but we do not know yet whether they will agree.

This Tour is some distance off yet, but it would be of considerable assistance to my Board if they could know whether, in the event of your being fit and being invited to captain the side, you will be prepared to do so. My Board have been given to understand that there will be no difficulty in obtaining the necessary permission from England for you to play for India.

*Needless to say, my Board hope that you will
find it possible to take active part on behalf of
India in its present efforts to take its place in
International Cricket fixtures.*

*Yours faithfully,
Grant Govan* (signature)
President.

After much activity behind the scenes the
Maharajah of Patiala was announced as captain
of the 1932 Indian team to tour England, to the
dismay of the Maharajah of Vizianagram. A
fortnight after the team had been announced
Patiala withdrew to be replaced by another prince,
this time of Porbandar. His qualifications as a
player were unconvincing as he showed with his
first five innings in which he scored a total of six
runs. He did not play again on the tour and a
"commoner", CK Nayudu, their outstanding
player, was appointed as captain for India's first-
ever Test. Indian cricket being what it was, this
caused dissension and jealousy as many of the
team resented one of their number being
appointed over them - a prince, yes, but a
commoner, no. Nayudu was the senior member
of a leading Indian cricket family and did not play
his last first-class game until the age of 68 in
1963/64. He had already come to the notice of
English cricketers when in Bombay on Gilligan's
1926/27 MCC tour he had hit 153, including the
then record in an innings of eleven 6s, for the
Hindus. His contributions on this tour were to
head the batting averages with the very

respectable average of 40.45, with five centuries, and to take 65 wickets. He came to England again in 1936 when he once more scored over 1,000 runs.

Perhaps all of this could have been avoided if the Nawab of Pataudi had not followed Duleep's example in refusing the captaincy. In his later period as a selector Duleep was to become more and more familiar with the machinations and internal politics of the game in India.

15.

DULEEP'S PLACE IN CRICKET HISTORY

THAT DULEEP WAS one of the finest batsman to be seen in the history of English cricket there can be little doubt. The volume of runs that he scored is only part of the story, important though this is. It is the manner in which he made them that ensures his name lives on over seventy years after his final innings. He had the benefit from his early school days at Cheltenham of immediately attracting attention as he was the nephew of KS Ranjitsinhji, the most glittering batsman in the so-called Golden Age of cricket in the late Victorian, early Edwardian era, although this could have been a drawback. Throughout his career there were inevitably comparisons made, a fact which in itself was a great compliment. Although he himself would never consider himself in the same class, many others did, with no less a player than Jack Hobbs saying he was even better. He was considered to be the finest schoolboy cricketer of his time in the early 1920s which caused his entry to Cambridge to be eagerly awaited by the cricketing world. He did not disappoint and in 1925 EHD Sewell, who could be a most vitriolic critic, was moved to write after seeing him score 53 against Yorkshire that "in him we have the best batsman seen since the war." He was impressed by his ability to score off anything at all loose, not that there would be too much of this from the White Rose attack! In view of later comments on his style it is surprising to read Sewell's opinion that he showed an inability to cut because of his stance; however, he did show prescience when he forecast that Duleep, who had confessed his limitations here, would soon be an expert in this area. Another person to write glowingly of the young Duleep's promise was that fine Lancashire and England bowler, Cecil Parkin. He thought that if he continued to improve as he was doing, he could become as famous as his uncle. He had sought the opinion of several eminent Yorkshire players, all of whom agreed that they were highly impressed with the mastery of so many strokes, which he had shown in the innings which had so impressed Sewell. Duleep was a born batsman and Sussex were very lucky to have such a "gem" coming to them. AC MacLaren, the former Lancashire and England captain, also spotted his potential at an early stage. He saw in him a young player who afforded the greatest amount of pleasure in watching him bat. Duleep was a player who stood alone among the younger players as a class batsman who would be able to score runs quickly enough to give England victory in English conditions.

Expectations were, therefore, extremely high, his progress closely followed as his brilliant career took shape. The great question is, of course, just how good would he have been and what would he have achieved given good health. That he had to retire through illness at the early age of 27 was a tragic loss to the game and to his countless admirers. There were periods during a season when he would have disappointing spells and it may be too simple to dismiss these just as the result of ill-health, although there is no doubt that fatigue, coughing up blood, chest pain, breathing difficulty and weight loss, all symptoms of his complaint, would be a great handicap for a man playing top-class sport! So great was his affliction that he finished up with having only half a lung. In an age of some of the finest batsmen seen in English cricket, he stood at the peak in his prime with only Herbert Sutcliffe and Walter Hammond to compare with him. In his great years of 1929 to 1931 he scored more runs than any other player in English cricket and if he had been able to accompany the 1932/33 team to Australia, Pelham Warner felt that this would have been the best England side ever to go there. In the opinion of EW Swanton only the extreme shortness of his career prevented him from being compared with Hammond, Hutton and Compton in an overall career assessment. He was finished at 27, whereas most players are in their prime between 25 and 35.

His lamentably short Test career served merely as a tantalising sample of what could have been expected from one of his talents over a reasonable period of time. His one Test against South Africa in 1929 was one of failure, but his non-selection for the rest of the series, in spite of being in such brilliant form during the season, was shameful. There seems little doubt that behind the scenes the politics of apartheid were responsible, whilst there remains some uncertainty behind the reasons for his not being a member of the MCC side to South Africa in 1930/31; to be charitable, perhaps it was decided that he would benefit more from a further trip to Switzerland. His seven Tests against New Zealand over two series were extremely successful as he finished with an average of over seventy with a century in each of the series. It is, however, against Australia that one is usually measured and in this respect Duleep emerged with flying colours. Apart from his 173 at Lord's, dealt with earlier in detail, he scored a further two half-centuries and two late forties in the series to give him the excellent average of 59.42. As in Ranji's case, he just failed to reach 1,000 runs in Tests with 995 at a very high average of 58.52.

Other batsmen may have had equally impressive records, but what was it then that made him so special? All who saw him or who played with him seemed to have been completely enchanted with his stroke-play, from the most experienced of fellow-cricketers, contemporaries and ex-players, and the most respected of critics, to spectators, connoisseurs and the more unsophisticated alike. He was elegance personified at the wicket with a variety of strokes in all directions, effortless drives, glances reminiscent of Ranji, all seemingly played with time to spare, with perhaps the late-cut being the one that brought most gasps from the enthralled onlookers. Denzil Batchelor wrote that no player since Ranji had "touched batsmanship with the lustre of magic as effortlessly as

Duleepsinhji". Showing his love of music as well as cricket, the legendary Neville Cardus posed the rhetorical question of whether a Caruso or a Gigli took a crowd nearer to true beauty than a Woolley or Duleepsinhji. PF Warner's view, poetically expressed, was that he had written his name in letters of gold in the greatest of all games. To AG Moyes he was an artist, a batsman of distinction and one of the most accomplished players he had ever seen. To John Marshall, author of *Sussex Cricket*, he was "an exquisite artist with a cricket bat". Writer AA Thompson also uses the same comparison describing him as "an elegant artist". Although a prolific scorer, he was never a hoarder of runs for their own sake, but believed in art and entertainment, which does not mean to say that he could not defend or fight when the situation demanded. Certainly he was no dilettante as he took the game seriously and was a fine team-player. Ian Peebles described him as having an orthodox and impeccable technique, but as with all truly great batsmen, he added strokes and refinements denied to those who were merely good.

It is interesting to read what his opponents and teammates thought of him. That great stylist Frank Woolley, with whom he is often compared, saw him at close quarters as an opponent and a teammate in two of his most celebrated matches. Playing for Kent in 1929, Woolley was on the field at Hastings when Duleep scored his 115 and 246 for Sussex and was a member of the England side at Lord's in 1930 when Duleep scored his famous 173. He was particularly impressed with his placement, with only Don Bradman to equal him, and, ironically, considering Sewell's words in 1925, he considered he was without exception the best cutter of all the great players that he had seen. The great Kent wicket-keeper/batsman Leslie Ames was also on the field at Hastings and recalled many years later his complete mastery over the Kent attack and the speed of his scoring. Ames pointed out that at the time Kent were leading in the championship, but the mauling they received that day led to something of a collapse and they finished up eighth. Jack Hobbs said he was a real artist, just like Frank Woolley. That paragon of fielders, Learie Constantine, recalled the occasion when he was fielding at cover and Duleep's timing was such that he played a seemingly defensive stroke which raced past him to the boundary with no hope of his stopping it. Although Duleep with his exemplary footwork had a great reputation for playing spin-bowling, as Freeman amongst others would testify, Herbert Sutcliffe gave an interesting viewpoint: what would give him great pleasure as a spectator would be to see Don Bradman batting against slow bowling and Duleep against fast bowing, when his glides and cuts would be prominent. Don Bradman wrote in his tribute on hearing of his death in 1959 of his 173 at Lord's: "...a thrilling exhibition of batsmanship of the kind so rarely seen today and for which cricket today would be all the better. He was one of the greatest batsmen I ever saw." Coming from such a source, this judgement underlines Duleep's claim to immortality as a cricketer.

Every batsman has his " bogey" bowler who does not necessarily count amongst the greatest of the breed. Jack Hobbs had JWHT ("Johnny Won't Hit Today") Douglas as his particularly feared adversary. It is surprising, given Duleep's mastery of slow bowling, how successful against him was Australian slow/medium left-arm spinner Percy Hornibrook from Queensland. His is not a particularly well-known name, yet in the eleven innings he played against him in 1930 he dismissed him eight times, four times in the Tests, twice against HDG Leveson Gower's XI and once each against the MCC at Lord's and Sussex at Hove. As soon as Duleep came in, Australian captain Bill Woodfull would put Hornibrook on the alert! Charlie Parker of Gloucestershire, a similar type of bowler, also dismissed him over the years on eight occasions in only fourteen innings. It is probably true to say though that there were many more bowlers who looked upon Duleep as their "bogey" batsman!

Duleep's claim to greatness does not, however, rest merely on his batting skills, supreme as these were. He has also been recorded in the history of the game as one of its finest fielders, especially in the slips. He made a name for himself in this department from his early days at Cheltenham with his unusually developed powers of anticipation, quickness of reaction and ability to hold on to chances at whatever speed and however high or low the ball had travelled. The only criticism of him, which remained throughout his career, was that he tended to stand too close, a position favoured by another great slip-fielder, Ian Botham, in later years.

As he progressed into first-class cricket, his reputation grew with his possibilities of becoming a Test player greatly enhanced by his skills in the field. By the time he had established himself in the Sussex side after his years at Cambridge he was being compared with Walter Hammond, not only as the best up-and-coming batsman of the generation, but also as the outstanding slip-fielder in the country. Two of his catches in particular have often been described: the one to dismiss CS Dempster in the Christchurch Test of 1930 was notable for its athleticism, as moving swiftly to his right he leapt to take one-handed a hard edge from the bowling of Maurice Allom, his erstwhile Cambridge colleague, whilst the one to dismiss CV Grimmett in the Sussex v Australians game of 1930 was a fine example of his anticipation as he caught the wily spinner "almost under his nose" off a dead-bat shot. Perhaps it is apocryphal, but many recall a match at Hove when with all players and spectators looking towards the boundary for a lightning edge, Duleep calmly produced the ball having pocketed it in flight. AG Moyes wrote of his having "the sharpest of eyes", whilst TCF Prittie attributed his brilliance to "swift instinct and hyper-acute vision". EM Wellings likened him to a cat and was impressed with his great agility which he attributed to his Indian blood. He noted particularly his gifts for taking catches in the slips off balls dropping well short of him, which he felt few Englishmen would be capable of.

It is not only in the slips, however, that he excelled as he was also a brilliant out-fielder who covered the ground at speed and threw powerfully. It was noted in his second year at Cambridge in 1926 that his returns to the wicket were just as strong as those of the visiting Australians who are usually looked upon as being supreme in this department. In the 1930 Test at Trent Bridge, when he spent many hours in the field as twelfth man substituting for the injured Sutcliffe, he shone away from his customary position in the slips. Many were the plaudits he received for his outstanding picking-up and accurate returns to the wicketkeeper. Freddie Brown recalled an occasion when he was playing for Surrey against Sussex and drove the ball past Duleep at mid-off. He thought that Duleep, being usually a slip-fielder, may not have a particularly good throw as he turned for a third run. Duleep's throw on the turn from the boundary hit the stumps at the bowler's end on the full with Brown halfway down the wicket!

We must also consider his qualities as a captain and his powers of leadership. His last year at Cheltenham was his first real test in this aspect of the game, a test from which he emerged with a fine reputation. His own outstanding playing ability naturally gained him great respect, but his qualities went beyond this. He had a great understanding of the game, he was able to motivate his team by understanding them as individuals and he showed he had the courage to make difficult decisions as in the case of one of his opening batsmen, Nigel Sharpe. Sharpe had been a stalwart of the side, but after having been hit on the head he had lost his confidence when facing pace bowlers, not an ideal situation for an opener! He would dearly have loved to have been chosen for the forthcoming match with Haileybury at Lord's, the most important match of the season for Cheltenham. However, after giving Sharpe several opportunities to overcome this fear, Duleep decided with heavy heart that he had to leave him out.

Duleep then went on to Cambridge where his character and ability should certainly in normal circumstances have ensured the award of the captaincy in his final year of 1928. His serious illness in 1927, which had caused him to miss most of the season and make a late start to the following year, would have naturally been a factor in his not being appointed captain, but there were also disturbing rumours that race had played its part.

Fortunately there were no such inhibitions with Sussex and they duly appointed him captain in 1931 to take over from Harold Gilligan. Any hesitation he may have felt upon receiving the invitation in Switzerland was immediately overcome when his uncle told (or perhaps commanded!) him unequivocally to accept it. Although he had one or two disappointing early season games, his form generally was excellent as he scored twelve centuries, his highest-ever number in a season. Sussex responded to his leadership as they rose from seventh to fourth in the championship. As in his schooldays, his own brilliance as batsman and fielder was a great asset in winning the loyalty of his players, but even more important perhaps were his personality, charm and sympathetic understanding of them as individuals. He made each player realise what his role was in the side and insisted on a settled batting order, which makes it easy to understand why he was so critical of Indian captains Pataudi and Amarnath in the 1940s for their inability to keep to a consistent order. He had this optimism that the side was good enough to be serious candidates for the title as the talent was there, but to succeed his task was to make the team into a unit which really believed in itself and in which each man would contribute selflessly. His skills in field placing and tactical assessments of the situation were widely remarked upon. John Marshall in *Sussex Cricket* calls him a great leader, whilst one of his leading players, Bert Wensley, said he never spared himself or his side; although it was hard work, it was of the kind that one really enjoyed.

With their improvement in 1931 even greater progress was expected in 1932, but as related in the opening chapter, this was at a high price. Sussex did indeed rise two places to become runners-up and for most of the season challenged Yorkshire, the eventual champions, very closely. It was too costly, however, as Duleep, driving himself on, continuing to be an inspiration as their leader and star player, collapsed under the strain at Taunton in mid-August, never to be seen again as a player. As Jim Swanton described him, "one of the most gifted as well as most graceful players who ever played for England".

He had already achieved undying fame as a batsman and as a fielder and there seems little doubt that had he been able to continue, he would have become one of the legendary captains in the annals of cricket.

16.

DULEEP'S PERSONALITY

KUMAR SHRI - Honourable Prince - Duleepsinhji was a person whose character made as great an impact as his cricket. It is very difficult to read about him as a player and in so many other of the roles he played in life without being made continually aware of the effect his charm, gentlemanly disposition and modesty had on all those whom he met. In fact, one eminent critic recalled his charm before his cricketing talent, a sentiment echoed by so many.

AG Moyes thought of him as an extraordinarily modest person, one who would live in one's thoughts as a gentle man and a gentleman. He called him "the most perfect gentleman I have known", a man extraordinarily modest and very self-critical. After having paid tribute to his cricketing skills, AA Thompson said he believed him to be what every boy would want his favourite cricketer to be, "modest and unaffectedly charming". PF Warner spoke of his good temper and good manners, attributes which made it "certain that there have been few cricketers more genuinely liked than Duleepsinhji". Jack Hobbs was impressed by how modest and unassuming he was, whilst Don Bradman's admiration was such that he felt "no finer gentleman or ambassador had ever trod the turf". To Leslie

Ames he was one of the most likeable and friendly cricketers ever to play for England. Old Cliftonian, RFS Talyarkhan, who played against him in school matches, wondered if any other Cambridge cricketer had ever been as popular, as he had a smile and a word for everyone. Such was his personality that if there were news of his batting at Fenner's, the crowd would rapidly grow. Prolific Australian batsman Bill Ponsford, who played in the 1930 series, called him a true sportsman and a thorough gentleman, one whose modest and unassuming manner endeared himself to all. RC Robertson-Glasgow, Oxford "Blue" and Somerset cricketer, who became an eminent journalist, described him thus: "Quiet, discerning and witty in conversation, yet he knew exactly how good he was and compared his powers without vain modesty (an interesting oxymoron!) or silly envy with those of the few great batsmen of the day."

There is one famous occasion, however, during his career when he was very angry and with unusual boastfulness promised revenge! The year was 1929 when he answered what he perceived to be Kent's doctoring the wicket at Maidstone to suit Freeman with the promise to score two centuries at Hastings in the return match. This he did with the bonus of a double century in the second innings. There was also a certain amount of arrogance in his Cambridge days when he told SMJ Woods, ex-Somerset captain, that he could play his county's bowling with a toothpick, so weak was the side they turned out. He scored 130 but said that he hardly counted this as a century. He was often quoted as being dismissive of hundreds scored against what he considered to be weak attacks and would talk more enthusiastically of moderate scores against class bowling in difficult conditions.

It is obvious that Duleep made a most favourable impression on all those who came into contact with him and all those who only knew him from afar. With all these tributes there could be a danger in thinking that he was a very paragon, one whose benign smile and courteous manner would be the answer to everything. There was more to his character than this, dominant though these features were. As demonstrated above, there could be a touch of arrogance about him and he knew he was a good player, unless his uncle was watching, that is. Duleep was very human and could show frustration and be very angry if he felt injustice. He could be impatient with those he felt were unworthy of office or who did not live up to his high ideals. When India were just starting to emerge as a Test-playing nation, he almost retired from the game when he was at the height of his powers as he felt that he was being used as a pawn in Indian cricket politics. He was confused as he just did not know where his loyalties lay - with his native country, with his adopted country or with his uncle's views? As a result then and later, when he returned to India he gave vent to some rather intemperate remarks at the expense of the Indian Board of Control, the President Grant Govan, and the Secretary Anthony de Mello in particular. He felt that for whatever reason he was being excluded from the higher echelons of the game when all he wanted to do was use his experience to help. The remarks he made to these two in his anger were untypical of him. He rounded aggressively on Govan for not having played at any respectable standard and spoke most sarcastically of de Mello's prowess as a bowler, which was of course totally irrelevant. He was indignant that rumours were circulating that he was seeking personal glory and had previously rejected the possibility of captaining India because England was a stronger side. In view of all the work he did in trying to encourage youngsters to participate in cricket he was also hurt by innuendo that he did not show enough interest in the game in his native country, which again he answered with strong language.

His periods as a selector did not always run smoothly with spells when he was out of office, not of his own choosing. Shortly after the Australian Services visit of 1945/46 when Duleep had been the Chairman, the selectors were convened to choose the Indian side and officials for the 1946 tour of England. A meeting marked by rancour and much politicking ended with Duleep being voted off the committee. Evidence was uncovered of an anti-Bombay coup which had made Pataudi captain rather than Vijay Merchant. The "plot" against Duleep so enraged one of the members of the Board that he refused to attend any further meetings. His career as a selector had certainly not run as he would have wished: his first spell had ended when he had had to temporarily resign through ill-health, his second had been marked with problems with Mushtaq Ali and Merchant, two of his country's most prominent cricketers. Perhaps, in retrospect, he could have handled affairs differently and not lost his temper on both occasions, and now when recalled to the colours he had been forced off the committee.

He also had an altercation with Pataudi in the weeks before the side left for England. Captaining North Zone against East Zone in one of his rare appearances in Indian cricket, Pataudi did not bat until No.8 and then declared after one ball when there was a large crowd, eager to see him bat. An angry Duleep accused him of shirking his responsibilities to which an even angrier Pataudi retorted with the words: "You of all people to say I shirked my duty. Go to the Ganges, dig up the ashes of your uncle Ranji and ask him what he thought of me." This incident did little credit to either of these two princes.

Whilst he was on the committee he had again shown his ability to spot talent at an early stage. He had championed the cause of the then unknown Amar Singh and Mankad, who had become great cricketers, and now he had discovered the potential of another fine player. When watching a trial at Bombay for the 1946 team, Duleep instantly saw in Fazal Mahmood the best medium-pace bowler in India since Amar Singh, but he was over-ruled and lesser bowlers such as Sohoni and Banerjee were selected. After partition Fazal became Pakistan's first great Test bowler, forever remembered for his part in his country's historic first Test win against England at the Oval in 1954 with figures of 6-53 and 6-46.

As seen in charting his career as a journalist, he also had an unfortunate relationship with another of India's greatest cricketers, Lala Amarnath. He had not been won over by Duleep's legendary charm when India's captain in Australia 1947/48 as he perhaps felt undermined by his advice which would have been given with the best of intentions.

At this distance of over seventy years one feels when reading of his relationship with his uncle that he could have stood up to him a little more. It must have been a little confusing for him to have Ranji build him up only to knock him over again. Duleep was not a conceited person, in fact we know he was generally very modest, so it was not a case of making sure the boy did not become too arrogant and over-confident. Duleep was a very intelligent person, but he seemed in total awe of his uncle, even to the extent of playing what proved to be his final match at Taunton. In spite of all his friends on the spot and medical experts who advised him not to play, Duleep succumbed to the taunts of his uncle from distant France. One can only conjecture how much more cricket he could played if he had but taken a short rest, but "uncle" had the last word. There is no doubt that Duleep owed an enormous amount to Ranji, in financial and in other ways, but there were times when one would wish that he had shown a little more independence.

To try to look objectively on the evidence presented there can be little doubt that Duleep was essentially a very charming person who had the ability to endear himself to those around him and to his multitude of admirers. His qualities shone in the many spheres of life he entered, from college study in Cheltenham to High Commissioner's chambers in Canberra, from the cricket field to the debating halls of state government in India; nor must we forget the great courage he demonstrated in his various careers whilst fighting his dread disease. If we can use one word to sum up most of the character defects, it would have to be pride, with at times a certain "prickliness" and sensitivity. It was this that caused his problems with the Indian Board of Control and with some of his country's star players, and it was pride which led to examples of arrogance in his younger playing days.

17.

FINALE

DULEEP"S LIFE came to a peaceful end on December 5, 1959, when he died in bed in his Bombay home. He had just played a leading part in setting up the All-India Sports Institute and a week before he had accepted the honorary Directorship. His commitment was such that he had been working on the project the day before his death. Aged only 54, he was tragically young and so obviously still had much to offer. The tuberculosis against which he had fought so hard for over thirty years finally claimed him. He had been keenly anticipating the arrival of the Australians for their 1959/60 tour and to renewing his friendship with them. As Robertson-Glasgow had said on his retirement, "It is a tale of concentrated glory, sad but triumphant."

The tributes paid to him as a cricketer and a person came from all parts of the cricketing world and from many politicians. Australian statesmen such as Dr. Evatt, Walter Crocker and Richard Casey were fulsome in their praise of him as politician and gentleman. Arthur Mailey said he was thankful not to have had to bowl at him in Tests; the Secretary of the MCC, Ronnie Aird, spoke of his endearing nature; Denis Compton said that the whole world would mourn his passing and the Australian captain in the 1930 series, Bill Woodfull, praised his fair-mindedness. All the major newspapers carried long obituaries and details of his achievements on and off the field.

Especially moving words are those from Don Bradman and from the Sussex handbook of the time. Bradman felt that "We are the richer for his brief but glorious tenure on earth", while the handbook states simply that "Wherever he played he was a true adornment".

To honour his passing there were two minutes' silence at the beginning of the first Test between India and Australia at Delhi on December 12.

As was to be expected, the *Wisden* of 1960 paid full tribute to the outstanding contribution he had made to cricket in the short career he was allowed. All his great triumphs were recalled from school days to Test matches with reminders of his prowess with the ball at Cheltenham. There was great emphasis placed on his personal qualities and popularity with his fellow players.

Perhaps the last words can be left with AA Thompson: " (Duleep) reminded players and spectators alike that cricket is first and foremost a beautiful game."

CAREER RECORDS

Season	Mtchs	Inns	NO	Runs	HS	100	50	0	Avge
1924	4	7	0	253	120	1	0	0	36.14
1925	15	29	2	1,056	130	2	8	2	39.11
1926	26	44	3	1,421	132	3	7	1	34.65
1927	3	5	1	434	254*	2	0	1	108.50
1928	22	39	3	1,706	198	6	7	2	47.38
1928/29(Ind)	1	2	0	122	84	0	1	0	61.00
1929	29	51	3	2,545	246	8	11	3	53.02
1929/30(Aus)	5	10	1	349	68	0	3	1	38.77
1929/30(NZ)	8	12	3	541	117	1	4	0	60.11
1930	29	48	3	2,562	333	9	6	2	56.93
1931	35	51	2	2,684	162	12	8	1	54.77
1931/32(Ind)	1	2	0	179	173	1	0	0	89.50
1932	27	33	2	1,633	132	5	9	2	52.67
Totals	**205**	**333**	**23**	**15,485**	**333**	**50**	**64**	**15**	**49.95**

TEST MATCHES

Season	Mtchs	Inns	NO	Runs	HS	100	50	0	Avge
1929(SA)	1	2	0	13	12	0	0	0	6.50
1929/30(NZ)	4	6	2	358	117	1	2	0	89.50
1930(Aus)	4	7	0	416	173	1	2	0	59.42
1931(NZ)	3	4	0	208	109	1	1	0	52.00
Totals	**12**	**19**	**2**	**995**	**173**	**3**	**5**	**0**	**58.52**

COUNTY CHAMPIONSHIP

Season	Mtchs	Inns	NO	Runs	HS	100	50	0	Avge
1926	12	21	1	696	132	2	3	0	34.80
1928	11	19	1	1,082	198	6	2	2	60.11
1929	21	36	0	2,028	246	7	9	2	56.33
1930	15	25	2	1,375	333	5	2	1	59.78
1931	23	34	2	1,857	162	9	5	1	58.03
1932	20	26	1	1,139	116	2	8	1	45.56
Totals	**102**	**161**	**7**	**8,177**	**333**	**31**	**29**	**7**	**53.09**

ALL MATCHES FOR SUSSEX

Mtchs	Inns	NO	Runs	HS	100	50	0	Avge
119	187	9	9,178	333	35	31	9	51.56

FOR CAMBRIDGE UNIVERSITY

Season	Mtchs	Inns	NO	Runs	HS	100	50	0	Avge
1925	11	21	2	932	130	2	8	1	49.05
1926	9	15	0	523	118	1	2	1	34.86
1927	3	5	1	434	254*	2	0	1	108.50
1928	9	16	1	444	96	0	3	0	29.60
Totals	32	57	4	2,333	254*	5	13	3	44.01

CENTURIES (50)

1924 (1)
120   MCC v Cambridge University at Lord's

1925 (2)
130   Cambridge University v Somerset at Bath
128   Cambridge University v The Army at Fenner's

1926 (3)
132   Sussex v Middlesex at Hove
118   Cambridge University v Free Foresters at Fenner's
115   Sussex v Hampshire at Hove

1927 (2)
254*   Cambridge University v Middlesex at Fenner's
101   Cambridge University v Yorkshire at Fenner's

1928 (6)
198   Sussex v Northamptonshire at Kettering
150   Sussex v Somerset at Weston-super-Mare
150   Sussex v Yorkshire at Eastbourne

125   Sussex v Middlesex at Hove
121   Sussex v Glamorgan at Eastbourne
107   Sussex v Kent at Hastings

1929 (8)
115
& 246 Sussex v Kent at Hastings
202   Sussex v Essex at Leyton
167*   MCC v Yorkshire at Scarborough
134   Sussex v Lancashire at Old Trafford
122   Sussex v Lancashire at Eastbourne
118   Sussex v Derbyshire at Hove
112   Sussex v Hampshire at Bournemouth

1929/30 (1)
117   ENGLAND V NEW ZEALAND at Auckland

1930 (9)
333   Sussex v Northamptonshire at Hove
188   Sussex v Hampshire at Portsmouth
185*   Sussex v Essex at Hove
173   ENGLAND V AUSTRALIA at Lord's
147   Sussex v Cambridge University at Fenner's
116
& 102* Sussex v Middlesex at Lord's
125
& 103* Gentlemen v Players at Lord's

1931 (12)
162   Sussex v Surrey at The Oval
161*   Sussex v Worcestershire at Dudley
140   Sussex v Essex at Chelmsford
133   Sussex v Essex at Hove
127   Sussex v Hampshire at Hastings
127   Sussex v Kent at Tunbridge Wells
112   Sussex v Leicestershire at Leicester
112   Sussex v Northamptonshire at Northampton

109   Sussex v Nottinghamshire at Horsham
109   ENGLAND V NEW ZEALAND at The Oval
103   Sussex v Middlesex at Hove
103   Sussex v New Zealanders at Hove

1931/32 (1)
173   Viceroy's XII v Roshanara Club and Visitors at Delhi

1932 (5)
132   Gentlemen v Players at Lord's
128   South v North at Old Trafford
126   Sussex v Surrey at Hove
116   Sussex v Worcestershire at Horsham
111   Sussex v Lancashire at Old Trafford

Duleepsinhji was top of the Sussex batting averages in every season in which he played i.e. 1926-1932.

His three greatest seasons with the bat were 1929-31 when he scored in total 7,791 runs, more than any other player in the country. These were also the seasons in which he held altogether 128 catches, exactly half of his career total of 256, with 47 in 1929 being the best.

INDEX

People

Grounds & Towns

209

Bodies in India associated with Duleep

Schools, Colleges & Universities

Books & Publications

BIBLIOGRAPHY

The author found the following books and publications particularly useful in doing research for his book *Duleepsinhji: Prince of Cricketers.*

Bose, Mihir,
History of Indian Cricket (1990)
Docker, Edward,
History of Indian Cricket (1976)
Frindall, Bill,
Wisden Book of Test Cricket 1877-1984 (1985)
Hammond, Walter,
Cricket My World (1948)
Lee, Christopher,
Official History of Sussex County Cricket Club (1989)
Roberts, Rex and Wilde, Simon,
Duleepsinhji, His Record Innings By Innings.
Various Writers,
Duleepsinhji, The Man and His Game (1963)
Warner, Pelham,
The Fight For The Ashes in 1930 (1930)
Wynne-Thomas, Peter,
Who's Who of Cricketers (1984)

In addition much use was made of the following:

Wisden
The Cricketer
Cheltonian magazine
Lady Clare magazine